THE
COUNTRY
HOUSE

———

BOOKS BY DONALD MARGULIES
AVAILABLE FROM TCG

Brooklyn Boy

Collected Stories

The Country House

Dinner with Friends

God of Vengeance

Luna Park: Short Plays and Monologues
INCLUDES:
July 7, 1994
Luna Park
Nocturne
Pitching to the Star

Shipwrecked! An Entertainment—The Amazing Adventures of Louis de Rougemont (As Told by Himself)

Sight Unseen and Other Plays
INCLUDES:
Found a Peanut
The Loman Family Picnic
The Model Apartment
Sight Unseen
What's Wrong with This Picture?

Time Stands Still

THE
COUNTRY
HOUSE

DONALD
MARGULIES

THEATRE COMMUNICATIONS GROUP
NEW YORK
2015

The publication of *The Country House*, by Donald Margulies, through TCG's Book Program, is made possible in part by the New York State Council on the Arts with the support of Governor Andrew Cuomo and the New York State Legislature.

TCG books are exclusively distributed to the book trade by Consortium Book Sales and Distribution.

Library of Congress Cataloging-in-Publication Data
Margulies, Donald.
The country house / Donald Margulies.
pages ; cm
ISBN 978-1-55936-491-1 (pbk.)
ISBN 978-1-55936-803-2 (ebook)
I. Title.
PS3563.A653C68   2015
812'.54—dc23   2014037558

Book design and composition by Lisa Govan
Cover collage by Donald Margulies

First Edition, January 2015

For Dana Morosini Reeve

THE
COUNTRY
HOUSE

Production History

The Country House was commissioned by Manhattan Theatre Club (Lynne Meadow, Artistic Director; Barry Grove, Executive Producer), with funds provided by U.S. Trust, and received its world premiere at the Geffen Playhouse (Randall Arney, Artistic Director; Ken Novice, Managing Director) in Los Angeles, CA, on June 11, 2014. It was directed by Daniel Sullivan; the set design was by John Lee Beatty, the costume design was by Rita Ryack, the lighting design was by Peter Kaczorowski, the original music was by Peter Golub and the sound design was by Jon Gottlieb; the production stage manager was Young Ji. The cast was:

SUSIE KEEGAN	Sarah Steele
WALTER KEEGAN	David Rasche
ANNA PATTERSON	Blythe Danner
ELLIOT COOPER	Eric Lange
MICHAEL ASTOR	Scott Foley
NELL MCNALLY	Emily Swallow

On October 2, 2014, this production of *The Country House* transferred to Broadway at the Samuel J. Friedman Theatre. It was produced by Manhattan Theatre Club in association with the Geffen Playhouse. The cast and personnel remained the same with the following exceptions: the sound design was by Obadiah Eaves, the production stage manager was James FitzSimmons, Michael Astor was played by Daniel Sunjata and Nell McNally was played by Kate Jennings Grant.

CHARACTERS

SUSIE KEEGAN, twenty-one, a college student, the plainly lovely daughter of a recently deceased actress named Kathy and

WALTER KEEGAN, sixty-six, a successful film and stage director; granddaughter of ANNA PATTERSON, the matriarch, a great and famous actress;

and niece of her late mother's brother, ELLIOT COOPER, forty-four, a failed actor and aspiring playwright.

MICHAEL ASTOR, forty-five, a ruggedly handsome, charismatic actor and longtime family friend.

It is the family's first gathering since Kathy's death, and Walter has brought along his new actress-girlfriend, NELL MCNALLY, early forties, an intelligent, inscrutable beauty.

SETTING

A house in the Berkshires. Summer.

Time

Act One

Scene 1: Friday afternoon
Scene 2: Later that night

Act Two

Scene 1: A few days later
Scene 2: Later that night

INTERMISSION

Act Three

Scene 1: The following morning
Scene 2: Later that day

Note

A slash " / " in the dialogue indicates the start of the next spoken line.

Act One

A century-old house in the Berkshires, near Williamstown, Massachusetts, that has long been the summer home of a family of theater people. Bought for a song four decades ago, it has changed relatively little over the years, and what improvements that were made were done piecemeal. Still, it is not without charm. Secondhand furnishings, collected over decades, somehow work in concert to convey cozy, Bohemian chic. (Look closely and you will see the decay.) Warped wooden shelves are crammed with mildewed, summer-reading paperbacks; arts-and-crafts made by two generations of children on rainy summer days; box games, a motley assortment of sporting equipment. Vintage posters from the Williamstown Theatre Festival and framed, faded production stills adorn the walls. Screened French doors open onto a brick patio and a garden. A kitchen, dining room and bathroom are accessible; a staircase leads to a warren of bedrooms on the second floor.

SCENE 1

A humid, overcast afternoon in early summer. Susie, barefoot in a black cotton dress, is curled up on the couch, looking through a photo album. Earbuds in, she's listening to Joni Mitchell and mumble-sings along the way people do when they can't hear themselves. We hear (but Susie does not) a car pull up on a gravel driveway.
Anna, sunglasses on, makes her entrance carrying canvas bags of groceries.

ANNA

(Entering) Darling, I can use a hand. *(Meaning: with the bags)*
Hello-o-o?

(Anna comes closer, startling Susie.)

SUSIE

God, Granna, / you almost gave me a heart attack!

ANNA

How do you expect to *hear* anything, those stupid things / in your ears?

SUSIE

You could have at least made your presence known.

ANNA

I entered the room. I am not one whose entrances go unnoticed. Except, apparently, by my own granddaughter.
Come here, you.

(Anna opens her arms to Susie, kisses the top of her head.)

You look more and more like your mother.

SUSIE

I look *nothing* like my mother.

ANNA

I haven't seen you in ages.

SUSIE

You saw me spring break.

ANNA

Thank you so much for opening the house.

SUSIE

You're welcome.

ANNA

The very thought of walking into this empty house . . .

SUSIE

I know.

ANNA

Something, isn't it? Rooms so alive with someone, once she's gone, all that's left is *stuff*.

(Susie brings the bags into the kitchen.)

When did you get here?

SUSIE

(Exiting) Last night. One of my suite mates gave me a ride from New Haven.

ANNA

(Calls) How can you wear black on a hot summer day? It makes me sweat to just look at you.

SUSIE

(Off) That's a fallacy, you know.

ANNA

Who said? Black is a heat magnet. And it's depressing.

(Susie returns.)

I need you to run lines with me later.

SUSIE

Do I have to? I read horribly.

ANNA

You do not. You read wonderfully. *(Remembers to ask)* Whose Porsche is sitting out there?

SUSIE

Dad's. Doesn't it just cry out "Male Menopause"?

ANNA

(Lower voice) Is he here? *(Meaning: upstairs)*

SUSIE

Went for a run.

ANNA

(Surprised) Your father's running?

SUSIE

See: Porsche above.

ANNA

Did he bring the girlfriend?

SUSIE

Oh, yeah. What kind of man brings his girlfriend to his dead wife's family's house? And what kind of woman goes *with* him?

ANNA

What's she like?

SUSIE

(Shrugs) Beautiful.

ANNA

And Elliot . . . ?

SUSIE

Uncle Elliot is napping. Uncle Elliot naps.

ANNA

Your Uncle Elliot naps . . . Far too much.

(She picks up a discarded liquor bottle.)

What are *you* doing inside on such a gorgeous day?

SUSIE

Waiting for *you*.

ANNA

Well, go! Shoo! Shouldn't you be out having unprotected sex with people your own age?

SUSIE

I'm with people my own age all year long.

ANNA

So, what? It's summertime! You know, I just got a look at some of this year's apprentices. They're adorable.

11

SUSIE

They're *always* adorable.

ANNA

You should hang out with them.

SUSIE

Why? They're all actors.

ANNA

What's wrong with actors?

SUSIE

I hate actors.

ANNA

You do not hate actors. Your whole *family* is actors.

SUSIE

Exactly.

ANNA

Very funny. Speaking of actors . . . Guess who I just ran into at Wild Oats.

SUSIE

Who?

ANNA

Michael Astor.

SUSIE

(Blushes) You're kidding. What was he doing there?

ANNA

He's doing a play / up here.

12

SUSIE

I know. What was he doing at Wild Oats?

ANNA

Shopping for food.

SUSIE

Michael shops for food? Doesn't he have like little assistants who run errands for him?

ANNA

Maybe in L.A. he does. He was by himself. Posing for people's iPhones.

SUSIE

That must've been a scene: Michael Astor in produce.

ANNA

I actually got a lot more looks than *he* did. I didn't recognize him right away; he's grown some sort of mustache.

SUSIE

Eew.

ANNA

He was supposed to move into his sublet today but there were bugs or something. They were going to put him in some *board* member's house—that awful woman with the high-decibel voice—I said absolutely not, he was staying *here*.

SUSIE

(Distressed) Here?!

ANNA

For one or two nights.

13

SUSIE

One or *two*?

ANNA

Until they can fumigate his sublet.

SUSIE

How could you *do* this to me?!

ANNA

What am I doing to you? You *love* Michael.

SUSIE

I *do* love Michael. In theory. And on television. That doesn't mean I want him staying in our *house* . . .

ANNA

I thought you'd be thrilled.

SUSIE

He's rich . . . Couldn't he stay at a hotel? What about The Williams Inn?

ANNA

Michael Astor is not going to stay at The Williams Inn—not when he has *us*.

SUSIE

The least you could have done was *ask* me first.

ANNA

Excuse me? This is still *my* house, young lady. I thought it would be *festive* having him here.

SUSIE

"Festive"?!

ANNA

Given the circumstances, yes. He'll be a welcome distraction.

SUSIE

(Vulnerably) But . . . I thought this was going to be, *you* know: just us. Immediate family.

ANNA

Oh, honey.

SUSIE

We were going to keep it low-key, look through photo albums and stuff.

ANNA

We *are* keeping it low-key.

SUSIE

No, now thanks to you we have guests to entertain. Michael, Daddy's girlfriend . . .

ANNA

Michael is hardly a guest who needs to be entertained.

(A car on gravel.)

SUSIE

Oh my God!

ANNA

Stop being such a drama queen.

SUSIE

I come by it genetically.

15

(Car door slams.)

Wait. Where's he gonna sleep?

MICHAEL

(Off) Hello?

SUSIE   ANNA

Shit.   *(Brightly)* In here!

(Michael enters with a leather duffle and a bag with bottles of wine and flowers. He indeed sports a mustache. Susie, blushing at the sight of him, tries to be invisible.)

MICHAEL

Anna.

ANNA

Michael. Welcome, darling. You remembered how to get here.

MICHAEL

Of course I remembered. These are for you.

(He kisses her cheek and presents her with the flowers.)

ANNA

Aren't you sweet! Thank you!

(He sees Susie for the first time.)

MICHAEL

That *can't* be little Susie . . .

ANNA   SUSIE

It certainly is . . .   *(Waves wanly)* Hi, Michael.

16

MICHAEL

The Susie *I* know is twelve years old. *Look* at you! Are you in college yet? / God, you must be.

SUSIE

Yes I'm in college; I'm practically a college *graduate*.

MICHAEL

Now I feel old. What are you majoring in?

SUSIE

Religious Studies with a minor in Psych?

MICHAEL

Interesting, coming from a family of heathen actors.

SUSIE

It's called reaction formation.

ANNA

Susie's the sane one. Always has been.

MICHAEL

Never got the acting bug?

SUSIE

You mean like scarlet fever? Or the plague?

ANNA

Ha.

SUSIE

Weren't you just in Africa?

MICHAEL

How did *you* know?

SUSIE

People magazine. It's not like it was a secret . . .

MICHAEL

Oh. Right.

ANNA

Were you shooting a movie or something?

MICHAEL

No no, I go a couple of times a year. To Congo, actually. We're building schools there.

ANNA

Oh, *that's* right . . .

SUSIE

Isn't that awesome? You've been doing it for a while now, right?

ANNA

Darling, why don't you see if Michael would like something to drink?

SUSIE

Michael, would you like something to drink?

MICHAEL

Why, yes, Susie, I would.

(He produces a bottle of Pellegrino from a bag.)

On ice? With lemon?

SUSIE

We don't have lemon.

(He presents one from the bag. Anna hands her the flowers.)

ANNA

I'll have the same, dear. Thanks.

SUSIE

Anything else? I'm like a little serf around here. All I need's
a little babushka.

ANNA

Shoo!

(She goes.)

MICHAEL

She's great.

ANNA

Susie? She's a rock.

MICHAEL

Elliot here?

ANNA

Napping, apparently.

MICHAEL

And Walter . . . ?

ANNA

Out running. *With* his new ladyfriend.

MICHAEL

Good for Walter.

ANNA

When do you start rehearsal?

MICHAEL

Tuesday. You?

ANNA

We follow you onto the Mainstage, so not for another three weeks or so.

MICHAEL

What are you going to do up here, take it easy?

ANNA

Learn my bloody lines, *that's* what! He used a lot of words, that Mr. Shaw.

MICHAEL

Back to Shaw.

ANNA

Yup.

MICHAEL

Which one?

ANNA

Mrs. Warren. I'm a tad long in the tooth for Mrs. W., but what the hell, it's summer theater. P.S. I'm terrified.

MICHAEL

Why? You're an old hand at this.

ANNA

Key word: "old."

MICHAEL

No . . .

20

ANNA

The noggin's not as reliable as it used to be, my dear. Just when I think I've got it down—*pffft!*—right into the ether.

MICHAEL

Happens to everybody.

(Anna has taken a framed photo off the wall to show him.)

Will you look at *that*: *Candida. How* many years ago?

ANNA

Twenty . . . four? What a marvelous Marchbanks you were.

MICHAEL

Look what a boy I was! I could be that boy's *father!*

ANNA

Don't talk to *me* about getting older. When you're *my* age, *you'll* still get the girl. *I'm* lucky if I get to play Grandma.

MICHAEL

I had such a crush on you . . .

ANNA

And every girl and boy was in love with *you.*

MICHAEL

I couldn't believe my good luck: playing love scenes with *Anna Patterson!*

ANNA

"Eugene: why are you so sad? Did the onions make you cry?"

MICHAEL

Your memory is going? Yeah, right.

21

ANNA

Lines I memorized twenty-five years ago are not the problem.

(She touches his face.)

"Poor boy! am I so cruel? Did I make it slice nasty little red onions?"

(They look at one another. Silence. A spark? Michael isn't sure. Susie, oblivious, returns with drinks.)

SUSIE

What's for dinner?

ANNA

They had these beautiful rib eyes; I thought we'd throw them on the grill.

SUSIE

(Sarcastic) Great.

ANNA

What.

SUSIE

I don't eat meat, remember?

ANNA

Oh of course.

SUSIE

How come nobody around here ever remembers I'm a vegetarian?

ANNA

I forgot. Forgive me.

SUSIE

It's hostile, Gran, / it really is.

ANNA

Oh, please. I can't keep track of all your fads.

SUSIE

"Fads"? I have a gluten allergy. A gluten allergy isn't a fad, it's a diagnosis. I *can't* eat gluten and I *don't* eat meat. What's so difficult to remember about that?

ANNA

Who even *heard* of gluten till a few years ago? *(To Michael)* Did you?

(He shrugs.)

Now it's the scourge of the nation.

MICHAEL

(Whispers, to Susie) I don't eat meat, either.

SUSIE

Ha! Michael doesn't eat meat, / either!

ANNA

You don't? How stupid of me! / I didn't think to ask.

MICHAEL

Don't worry. I'm sure there'll be plenty for me to eat. Hey, where should I put my stuff?

ANNA

Susie'll show you.

SUSIE

Where?

ANNA

I thought you could give Michael *your* room.

SUSIE

Oh.

MICHAEL

You don't have to do that . . . Where will Susie sleep?

ANNA

Down here. / On the couch.

MICHAEL

No, no, I'll sleep down here.

ANNA

She doesn't mind.

MICHAEL

I'm more than happy to sleep on the couch.

SUSIE

This is actually a much better deal, believe me: My bed sucks.

ANNA

You're not really going to let Michael / sleep in the living room . . .

MICHAEL

I don't mind! / Really!

SUSIE

He doesn't mind!

ANNA

Well, I'm not going to argue with you.

(Anna gives Susie a look as she exits to the kitchen.)

SUSIE

I hope you don't think I'm a brat. / 'Cause I'm really not.

MICHAEL

Not at all. I crashed many a night on this couch. Back in the old days. I'm kinda looking forward to it.

(Pause.)

I was crazy about your mother, I hope you know that.

SUSIE

I know. You were lovers.

MICHAEL

What?! Who told you *that*?

SUSIE

She did. Before she died she told me about *all* her lovers.

MICHAEL

Jesus. That must've been some conversation.

SUSIE

It was.

MICHAEL

We met *here*, you know. At Williamstown.

SUSIE

I know.

MICHAEL

Not much older than you are now.

SUSIE

Uh-oh. This isn't gonna be like *Mamma Mia* or something, turns out you're my real father?

MICHAEL

(Laughs) Uh, no. Not that I know of.

SUSIE

So what's with the mustache?

MICHAEL

What, you don't like it?

SUSIE

Truthfully?

MICHAEL

Yeah.

SUSIE

Looks stupid.

MICHAEL

(Amused) Stupid?!

SUSIE

You asked me what I / thought!

MICHAEL

Yeah, but "stupid"?!

SUSIE

Why'd you grow it?

MICHAEL

For the play I'm doing.

SUSIE

What play is it?

MICHAEL

The Guardsman.

SUSIE

Never heard of it.

MICHAEL

It's old. It's a comedy.

SUSIE

Is it funny? Or is it one of those old comedies that isn't funny?

MICHAEL

No, it's funny. Kinda. I wanted something light.

SUSIE

Your character has a mustache?

MICHAEL

It doesn't say specifically.

SUSIE

Then why did you grow one?

MICHAEL

That's how I saw him.

SUSIE

With a mustache.

MICHAEL

Yeah. It helps me find my character.

SUSIE

You need facial hair to find your character? That's lame.

MICHAEL

Why? Olivier loved noses, prosthetic noses . . .

SUSIE

Yeah, but that was Olivier.

MICHAEL

Thanks a lot.

SUSIE

No offense. I mean, who are you fooling? You're one of those actors, no matter what you do, you'll always be you.

MICHAEL

I'm not sure how I should take that . . .

SUSIE

I guess that's what it means to be a star.

MICHAEL

What.

SUSIE

You give people pleasure just by being *you*. They don't care what play you're in or what part you're playing, all they care about is seeing *you*. In the flesh. Like, when my grandmother walks out on stage?

MICHAEL

Yeah . . . ?

SUSIE

I love looking around at the audience. Everybody's beaming.
Just at the sight of her. They *love* her. You *feel* their love for
her. Give the people what they want.

MICHAEL

What.

SUSIE

You! Michael Astor! Not some character with a stupid mustache. Besides, you have a nice upper lip.

MICHAEL

You think I have a nice upper lip?

SUSIE

Oh, come on, you know you do. God.

MICHAEL

What.

SUSIE

Actors. You're all alike. No matter how beautiful and famous
you are . . .

(He laughs.)

What.

MICHAEL

You're funny.

SUSIE

Gee, thanks. What do *you* care what I think, anyway?

MICHAEL

I care very much.

SUSIE

Why?

MICHAEL

(Shrugs) I like you. I'm fond of you.

SUSIE

Eew.

MICHAEL

What.

SUSIE

"Fond."

MICHAEL

What's wrong with "fond"?

SUSIE

You're fond of dogs. Or Indian food. How do you know you're fond of me? You don't even know me.

MICHAEL

What do you mean I don't know you, I knew you in utero!

SUSIE

Yeah, but that's not the same as *knowing* me.

MICHAEL

You're a tough house, you know that?

SUSIE

So what happened with you and your girlfriend?

MICHAEL

What?!

SUSIE

Didn't you have like a bitter breakup?

MICHAEL

How do you know these things?!

SUSIE

It was like everywhere! What *is* it with you and those gorgeous skinny models, anyway?

MICHAEL

What do you mean?

SUSIE

They all have like this disturbingly wide gap between their legs / that doesn't even seem anatomically possible.

MICHAEL

Okay.

SUSIE

I mean, they're incredibly picturesque. But they don't seem very . . . I don't know, *substantial*. I guess substantial isn't what you're looking for, huh. You just want women who are functional and decorative . . .

MICHAEL

All right . . .

SUSIE

. . . I mean, if you were seriously looking for a wife and the mother of your children, you could have any woman in the world . . . But I guess you're not there yet. Look at my dad: He was like forty-five when I was born, so there's hope for you.

MICHAEL

(Quasi-amused) Who *are* you?

(Elliot comes downstairs.)

ELLIOT

Susie, why'd you let me sleep so late? / I *told* you to wake me up!

SUSIE

I'm sorry! I forgot! I was busy!

(She points to Michael.)

ELLIOT

Wow! Look who's here!

MICHAEL

Hey!

SUSIE

(Going upstairs, calls) Gran? Uncle / Elliot's up!

ELLIOT

I *heard* you were going to be up here . . .

MICHAEL

Drove up this afternoon.

(The men embrace.)

ELLIOT

(Regarding the mustache) What the fuck is *this*?

MICHAEL

It's just . . .

(Anna enters with a vase of flowers.)

ANNA

Hello, darling, have you rejoined the living?

(She offers Elliot her cheek, which he kisses.)

ELLIOT

Hello, Mother. Look who the cat dragged in!

ANNA

Not the cat, dear, little old me. I found him at the supermarket.

ELLIOT

The *super*market? With all us mere mortals?

MICHAEL

Fuck you.

ELLIOT

Where you staying?

MICHAEL

Here, apparently.

ELLIOT

(Unpleasantly surprised) Oh! *(Looks at Anna)* Wow!

MICHAEL

The house I was supposed to move into, they'd set off this toxic insect bomb in it; started choking the minute I walked in. So, until they can air the place out . . .

ANNA

(Returning to the kitchen) I *insisted* he stay with *us*!

33

MICHAEL

Persuasive woman your mother.

ELLIOT

You're telling *me.*

MICHAEL

Hey, I told your mom: I am so sorry I didn't make it to the thing for Kathy.

ELLIOT

That's all right. You sent flowers . . . and all that food . . .

MICHAEL

I should've been here.

ELLIOT

You were shooting. What actor wouldn't understand that? Kathy certainly would . . .

MICHAEL

I should've come last summer. I kept telling myself there'd be time.

ELLIOT

We all did.

MICHAEL

I'm one of those people who has a hard time with hospitals.

ELLIOT

(Faux analytical) And yet you play a doctor on TV. / Hm . . .

MICHAEL

I know. Ironic, isn't it?

34

ELLIOT

She died *here*, actually. *(Meaning: this room)*

MICHAEL

Oh.

ELLIOT

Put a hospital bed right here. Facing the garden. Just as she wanted. My beautiful sister. Gone.

MICHAEL

Unbelievable.

ELLIOT

I can't believe it and I was here when she died. "After a heroic battle with cancer." Isn't that what they like to say? *What* "heroic battle"? Cancer beat the living shit out of her.

MICHAEL

I'm sorry, man. I know what she meant to you.

ELLIOT

Thanks.

MICHAEL

Have you seen Walter?

ELLIOT

Is he here?

(Michael nods.)

Must have arrived while I was napping.

MICHAEL

Apparently he's out jogging.

35

ELLIOT

(Chortles derisively) Jogging?! He has a girlfriend. / Do you know he has a girlfriend, my brother-in-law?

MICHAEL

Uh-huh. So I heard. Have you met her?

ELLIOT

No, not yet. This is her debut.

MICHAEL

Ah.

ELLIOT

That didn't take very long, did it. My sainted sister barely in the ground and that son of a / bitch—

MICHAEL

(Calming) Now, now.

ELLIOT

How's *your* love life? No, don't tell me.

MICHAEL

I haven't been in love with anybody in a long time.

ELLIOT

Really? What about that last model-hyphen-girlfriend of yours?

MICHAEL

That was just . . . There are all these women parading through my life who are too willing, too accessible. Sometimes I feel like I'm being used for sex so they'll have a story to tell their friends.

(A beat.)

ELLIOT

Yeah, I *hate* when that happens.

MICHAEL

Yeah, well, a steady diet of that isn't very nourishing. You begin to feel not so good about yourself. How have *you* been?

ELLIOT

Well, I wasn't exploited for sex and luck into a hit series, if *that's* what you mean. You want to know what I *am* doing?

MICHAEL

What.

(A beat.)

ELLIOT

I'm writing.

MICHAEL

What do you mean?

ELLIOT

I'm writing!

MICHAEL

What are you writing?

ELLIOT

I'm writing a *play*, actually.

MICHAEL

A play! Really! A full-length play?

ELLIOT

Yes. A full-length play. Why? Is that so hard to believe?

MICHAEL

No, it's just, I didn't know you wrote plays.

ELLIOT

I didn't; this is my first.

MICHAEL

Congratulations.

ELLIOT

Well, not since I was twelve; Kathy and I would put on these little skits for the amusement of our mother, the queen. But this play: it's as if it had been inside me all along, it practically wrote itself. I've found my calling, Michael, I really have.

MICHAEL

Wow, that's exciting.

ELLIOT

You're the first person I've told so keep it on the q.t. I haven't had the guts to say it out loud before: I'm a playwright. I. Am. A playwright. I'm ready to give up acting.

MICHAEL

Really!

ELLIOT

Well, that's not entirely accurate: In order to give up acting I have to have *been* acting. Announcing that I'm ready to give up *auditioning* doesn't have quite the same impact.

MICHAEL

I'd love to read it. Can I?

ELLIOT

I'm almost done; I still haven't cracked the last scene.
It's good, Michael, I think it's really good.

MICHAEL

I'm sure.

ELLIOT

Why are you sure?

MICHAEL

You're a bright guy . . .

ELLIOT

Not every bright guy can write a good play.

MICHAEL

True. But you've been around theater all your life . . . It's in
the genes.

ELLIOT

Are you patronizing me?

MICHAEL

What? No! I'm trying to be encouraging! *(Smiling)* Jesus, Elliot,
what the—!

NELL

(Off, calls) HELLO? CAN SOMEONE HELP?!

*(Walter's ad-libbed off-stage protests are heard. Michael looks
at Elliot quizzically; Elliot shrugs.)*

WALTER

(Off) I can do it . . . It's not such a big deal . . . *(Etc.)*

(Michael runs out.)

MICHAEL

(Off) What's going on?

WALTER

(Off) Michael . . . !

MICHAEL

(Off) Walter!

(Walter enters being assisted by Michael and Nell. She and Walter are in running clothes. Elliot is stunned when he sees her.)

WALTER	ELLIOT
. . . Didn't expect to find *you* here.	*(Passively)* Mother? Susie? Something's wrong with Walter.

(Anna and Susie run out.)

ANNA	SUSIE
What happened?!	Daddy?!

(Overlapping introductions are made as Walter is ministered to by everyone but Elliot, who remains on the periphery.)

WALTER

Some entrance, huh? Anna!

ANNA

Hello, darling.

WALTER

Whataya know, the gang's all here.

SUSIE

Sit him down here.

NELL

I never should've let him run . . .

WALTER

It's my own damn fault.

SUSIE

Would ice help? I'll go get ice.

(Susie goes.)

WALTER

(To Susie) Thanks, / kiddo.

ANNA

(To Walter) What did you do to yourself?

WALTER

Fucking knee.

ANNA

Poor Walter. Why didn't you call? / We would've come to fetch you.

NELL	WALTER
We didn't have our phones.	Didn't take our phones.

(Susie returns with a bag of frozen peas.)

SUSIE

Well, that wasn't very smart, / was it.

ANNA

It was an emergency. You could've knocked on someone's door.

NELL

That's what I told him. He refused.

WALTER

My fucking knee went out! It's not like I had a heart attack . . .

SUSIE

What if you did?! You *could* have . . . !

NELL

Miss Patterson, I have to say . . . I am such a fan.

ANNA

Oh, thank you, dear. Tell me your name again?

NELL

Nell.

ANNA

Nell. Right.

MICHAEL

(Overlapping, attempting levity) I'm not a doctor, but I play one on TV . . . May I . . . ?

WALTER

Well, it's a little tender.

(Michael palpates Walter's knee.)

Ow!

MICHAEL

Sorry!

ANNA

I think I have Vicodin. You want a / Vicodin?

WALTER	ANNA
May not be a bad idea.	*(To Susie)* Go look in my
I should go lie down.	medicine cabinet.

(Susie runs upstairs ahead of Michael and Anna, who help Walter.)

MICHAEL

(Extending his hand) I'm Michael, by the way.

NELL

I know who you are. Nell McNally.

MICHAEL

Nice to meet you, Nell.

(Walter tries to get up.)

NELL

Oh, honey . . .

WALTER

Sorry to be such a gimp. Bet you never thought life with me would be so exciting.

NELL

I knew.

(As he goes past, Walter notices Elliot.)

WALTER

(Surprised) Elliot!

ELLIOT

Walter.

WALTER

I didn't see you there!

(Elliot waves in greeting.
Ad-libs as the others go upstairs.)

ANNA

Careful on the stairs, they're uneven . . .

MICHAEL

(Exiting) Walter, I never told you how sorry I was about Kathy.

WALTER

(Off) I know you were, champ.

(Elliot and Nell are alone. Silence.)

ELLIOT

(À la Bogart) "Of all the gin joints in all the towns in all the world . . ."

NELL

Hello, Elliot.

ELLIOT

So *you're* the new girlfriend. How do you like that?

NELL

How've you been?

ELLIOT

How've I been: Gee, let's see . . . Eleven years? A couple of years ago: Okay. Last year? Not so hot.

NELL

I'm sorry about your sister.

ELLIOT

Yeah, thanks.

NELL

I should have written you.

ELLIOT

That would have been nice.

NELL

I'm sorry I never got to work with her; she sure was a wonderful actress.

ELLIOT

Lucky for you, though, huh, Walter bein' a big Hollywood director an' all.

NELL

I should go see how / he is. *(Starts to go)*

ELLIOT

(Derisively) Jogging!

NELL

(Stops) What?

ELLIOT

The man is, what, sixty-six years old?

NELL

That's not old.

45

ELLIOT

Running around outside in his brand-new little jogging suit?
In ninety-degree heat?

NELL

It isn't ninety / degrees.

ELLIOT

He's lucky he didn't have a massive coronary. Or a devastating stroke.

NELL

He's an incredibly *vigorous* sixty-six year old, if you ask *me*.

ELLIOT

I *didn't*. Ask you.

(Pause.)

Where've you been?

NELL

I moved to L.A.

ELLIOT

(À la Palin) How'd that work out for ya?

NELL

Episodic work here and there, a few pilots that didn't get picked
up . . .

ELLIOT

How is it possible?

NELL

What.

ELLIOT

You're lovelier than ever.

NELL

I'm not.

ELLIOT

Eleven years, for you, have been a gift.

NELL

Hardly.

ELLIOT

Time . . . has only *toyed* with *me*, made me more foolish. You . . . ?
Only more exquisite. *(Pause)* Nellie . . .

NELL

Don't.

ELLIOT

Did all those weeks in Louisville . . .

NELL

Elliot . . .

ELLIOT

. . . doing that *terrible* play . . . mean nothing?

NELL

Of course not.

ELLIOT

We were inseparable! Every day for weeks! On stage and off!

NELL

We made the most of a bad situation, that's all; made it *bearable* / for each other.

ELLIOT

No no, more than that, more than just bearable: *Bliss.*

NELL

Bliss?

WALTER

(Off, from upstairs) Nell?

NELL

(Calls) Yes? Need anything?

WALTER

(Off) Only you.

NELL

(Calls) Be right there.

ELLIOT

Tell me something: When you took up with Walter . . . I'm curious; this is fascinating. Surely you knew he and I were related.

NELL

Of course I knew.

ELLIOT

Did you even bother telling him about Louisville . . .

NELL

Yes.

ELLIOT

. . . or was it such an insignificant blip in your life it wasn't worth / mentioning?

48

NELL

No, I told him.

ELLIOT

So when you knew you were coming here, you didn't think *preparing* me might have been the right thing to do?

NELL

"Preparing" you?

ELLIOT

A postcard? An email? "By the way, I'm fucking your dead sister's husband"?

NELL

Don't be disgusting.

(She starts for the stairs; he follows.)

ELLIOT

Hey . . .

NELL

Frankly, I didn't feel I owed you an explanation.

ELLIOT

Oh, really? Why's that?

NELL

We were *colleagues*, / Elliot.

ELLIOT

Colleagues! We *weren't* just "colleagues" . . . ! *(Sudden and piercing) I loved you!*

49

WALTER

(Off, from upstairs) Nell?

ELLIOT

I was in love with you!

NELL

You have to make peace with this, Elliot. Walter's asked me to marry him, and I told him I would. Now if you'll excuse me, we'll see you at dinner.

(She goes upstairs leaving him dumbfounded.)

Scene 2

Later. Dusk. Elliot, wearing a "kiss the cook" apron, enters from the patio, followed by Michael, who has shaved off his mustache.

ELLIOT

It's the first anniversary! That's why we're here!

MICHAEL

Shhh . . .

ELLIOT

(Lowers voice) Does my mother suggest that maybe it's not such a good idea to bring the girlfriend? No! "Bring her along!" she says. Why? Because she *loves* Walter. Like a son, she says. Never mind they're practically the same age . . .

MICHAEL

She *is* beautiful, the girlfriend . . .

ELLIOT

"Beautiful"? "Beautiful" is too banal a word for what she is. "Radiant" is what she is. "Incandescent."

MICHAEL

Okay. What's the story?

ELLIOT

The story is . . . there *is* no story. I could have had her, I let her get away. The end.

MICHAEL

When?

ELLIOT

Eleven years ago. We did a play together. In the Humana Festival. You ever been to Louisville in February?

(Michael shakes his head.)

We were like sole survivors of a nuclear winter. Clung to one another for dear life. Breakfast, rehearsals, drinks after the show. Did everything but sleep together. It was like—

MICHAEL

You didn't sleep together?

ELLIOT

Sometimes we slept in the same bed but, no, we never *slept together*–slept together.

MICHAEL

Why not?

ELLIOT

She had a boyfriend back in New York.

51

MICHAEL

How many weeks?

ELLIOT

Six?

MICHAEL

You shared a *bed* with this . . . "incandescent, radiant" woman . . .

ELLIOT

I know, how quaint, right?

MICHAEL

. . . for *six* weeks . . .

ELLIOT

Not *every* night . . .

MICHAEL

. . . and you never slept with her?!

ELLIOT

I was ecstatic just to *be* with her. If you can imagine such a thing. Talking. For hours on end. Laughing. She has the most joyful *laugh*, Nell. Making her laugh was one of the greatest pleasures of my life. Seeing her now?, with *him*?, you'd never know she was *capable* of such joy.

(We hear voices on the stairs. Michael signals for Elliot to quiet down.)

Fuckin' vampire. Sucked the life-force right out of her.

(Nell helps Walter down the stairs.)

WALTER

Not too late to trade me in for a younger model, you know.

NELL

Not a chance.

WALTER

Why should you be saddled with an old man?

NELL

I'll be old soon enough. Watch: Five years, the bloom'll be off the rose.

WALTER

'L never happen.

(He kisses her cheek.
Anna enters from the kitchen and hands Elliot a platter.)

ANNA

Elliot?

(Elliot takes the platter and goes out to the grill. Anna returns to the kitchen.)

MICHAEL

How's the patient?

NELL

Upright.

WALTER

For the time being.

(Michael helps Nell get Walter settled into a chair.)

> NELL

Hey, didn't you have a mustache?

> WALTER

Oh, yeah!

> MICHAEL

Susie talked me out of it . . .

> WALTER

(Referring to the ottoman) Susie, honey, could you uh . . . ?

> NELL

(Continuous, to Michael) I like this better.

> MICHAEL

I do, too.

(Susie moves the ottoman closer so that Walter can elevate his leg.)

> WALTER

Thanks, kid.

(She starts to go. He takes her hand to stop her.)

Hey. How's my girl?

> SUSIE

(Unsmiling) Awesome.

(Susie brusquely pulls her hand away as she goes. Michael opens wine, serves. Anna enters from the kitchen with a bowl of nuts.)

> NELL

(To Anna) I love your house.

ANNA

Yeah? Don't look too close. It's sort of like me: It needs work.

WALTER

I was telling Nell about this house, teeming with actors, all summer long, year after year. Everybody came to Anna's.

NELL

Sounds fabulous.

ANNA

It had its moments.

MICHAEL

I even *remember* some of them.

(Anna makes room on the couch; he joins her.)

WALTER

(To Michael) Hey, I haven't seen you since your series took off!

NELL

Yes, congrat / ulations!

MICHAEL

Oh, yeah, thanks.

ANNA

I didn't realize it was still on the air.

SUSIE

Still?! It's huge!

MICHAEL

Just wrapped season three.

55

ANNA

I had no idea.

(Elliot returns from the patio with a foil-wrapped platter of steaks.)

MICHAEL

Damn thing's taken over my life: Our schedule is insane, and when I'm not shooting, they've got me promoting the show!

ELLIOT

You're not complaining, / are you?

MICHAEL

No . . .

ELLIOT

Because that would be in really bad taste.

(Elliot exits to the kitchen.)

MICHAEL

I used to think, if I only got a series . . . I'd have it made. I'd never have to worry about anything again.

NELL

Isn't that what every actor thinks?

ANNA

Are you an actress, dear?

NELL

Yes . . .

SUSIE

(Overlapping, to Anna) I told you that.

(Anna shrugs.)

NELL

I feel like such a fraud telling *Anna Patterson* I'm an actress.

ANNA

Aren't you sweet. Might I have seen your work?

NELL

Not unless you watch shows intended for preadolescent girls.
I went from "Hot Neighbor" to "Single Mom" seemingly over-
night.

(Elliot returns from the kitchen, lingers on the periphery.)

WALTER

Nell's a *wonderful* actress.

ANNA

Ah!

NELL

Walter . . . You don't know that . . .

WALTER

I've seen enough to know. She's just being modest.

ELLIOT

Isn't it funny how people always say that?

WALTER

What.

ELLIOT

"She's a *wonderful* actress." It's not enough to say that she's an
actress, no, she has to be a *wonderful* actress. As if the quality
of actress she is, is a reflection on *you*.

57

WALTER

In this case, it happens to be true.

ELLIOT

I know; we worked together.

WALTER

That's right!

ANNA

(Overlapping) You did? *(Nell nods)* When was that?

NELL

Years ago.

ELLIOT

Remember that play I did? In the Humana Festival?

ANNA

Vaguely.

ELLIOT

I did a play? Eleven years ago? In Louisville?

ANNA

I can't keep track of every play you've ever done.

ELLIOT

There haven't been that many.

ANNA

(To Michael) You're a detective or something? On your show?

SUSIE

(Shocked) Granna! Do you honestly not know?

MICHAEL

(Feigned offense) I'm Dr. Alec Matheson, chief of extraterrestrial medicine on Lunar Pod VI!

SUSIE

You know, Granna, going around saying how you don't watch TV . . . It's not even pretentious anymore . . .

ANNA

Why thank you, dear.

SUSIE

. . . it's just plain out of it.

ANNA

I know, everyone's always telling me all the great stuff I'm missing.

SUSIE

You are!

WALTER

You really are.

MICHAEL

Well, my show isn't one of them.

NELL

Oh, I like it.

MICHAEL

Why?

NELL

It's a guilty pleasure.

MICHAEL

Which is another way of saying it's not very good.

NELL

No . . .

(They share a laugh.)

ANNA

I hope it's made you rich.

MICHAEL

(Equivocal) It's made me rich . . .

ANNA

Good!

MICHAEL

The next two years'll make me *very* rich.

ANNA

Even better.

WALTER

And here you are, back in Williamstown, right on schedule.
Where *all* ambivalent successful actors come for absolution.

MICHAEL

Guilty.

WALTER

Return to their roots, remind themselves why they got into this
business in the first place, work their asses off—for nothing—
then fly home to Hollywood, cleansed and virtuous.
    The Williamstown Cure: Better than a high colonic! Cheers.

(He raises a glass and drinks. Michael does, too.)

MICHAEL

Cheers.

WALTER

What play are you doing up here / again?

MICHAEL

The Guardsman.

WALTER

Molnár.

MICHAEL

Right.

WALTER

Old chestnut.

MICHAEL

Young director.

ANNA

They're all young.

WALTER

So it seems.

ANNA

This boy director who's doing *Mrs. Warren* . . . Everyone was
telling me I *had* to work with him, how brilliant he is.

WALTER

Maybe he *is.* We were all young once.

ANNA

We shall see. *You're* so good with Shaw, darling. Remember the time we had on *Candida*? . . .

MICHAEL

Uh-huh.

WALTER

. . . I had a ball directing that show!

ANNA

You *must* give me notes on *Mrs. Warren.*

WALTER

Sure. Who's your Vivie?

ANNA

Some TV actress.

MICHAEL

Hey, watch it!

ELLIOT

I don't envy *her*. Mother eats ingenues for breakfast.

ANNA

I do not.

ELLIOT

It's true, Mother, you always choose a designated victim, on every production you work on, some underling you can project all your anxieties onto.

ANNA

That's a very uncharitable thing / to say . . .

ELLIOT

Usually the ingenue. Sometimes the dresser. The green p.a. working for nothing . . .

WALTER

So your boy director . . .

ANNA

You should see him! He barely shaves!

WALTER

You met with him?

ANNA

I had lunch with him at Orso.

WALTER

And?

ANNA

He was lovely, but so *serious*. Like a grave little prodigy.

WALTER

If you were so unsure about him, why'd you say yes?

ANNA

Because I had to, darling. I had to get back to work. It was time. It'd been a whole year since Kathy . . . Time to get back to the only thing I know how to do. I figured what better place than here? Either that or go insane.

WALTER

I know what you mean.

(A solemn silence, which Michael attempts to break.)

MICHAEL

I'm looking forward to reading *Elliot's* play.

(Elliot shoots him a look.)

ANNA

Play? What play?

MICHAEL

(Realizing his faux pas) Oh, shit.

WALTER

Elliot, have you written a *play*?

SUSIE

Have you, Uncle Elliot?

ELLIOT

(Daggers at Michael) Thanks a lot.

MICHAEL

(To Elliot) I'm sorry, I assumed it was common knowledge.

ELLIOT

Why would you assume *that*? I *told* you . . .

WALTER

I want to hear about this play!

NELL

Yes, tell us!

ELLIOT

There's nothing to tell. I'm writing a play.

WALTER

A full-length play?

ELLIOT

Yes, a full-length play.

ANNA

Isn't that wonderful.

ELLIOT

Two acts and everything. I even typed it myself. See? This is why I didn't want to tell you people.

ANNA

Who are you calling "you people"? We're your family! Since when are we "you people"?

ELLIOT

Since the day I was born?

ANNA

Oh, you.

ELLIOT

Everybody gets that tone with me.

ANNA

What tone?

ELLIOT

"A play! Wow! Isn't that marvelous!" Like I'm a moron or an out-patient or something.

MICHAEL

Jesus, Elliot . . .

SUSIE   ANNA

Oh, Uncle Elliot . . .   Oh, God . . .
.

WALTER

That's all in your head, champ.

ELLIOT

Oh, yeah? All in my head?

WALTER

I think it's *super* you've written a play.

ELLIOT

Super.

WALTER

Yes. I'm jealous. It's quite an accomplishment.

ELLIOT

You're jealous? Of me?

WALTER

That you actually had the discipline to sit down and write a full-length play? You bet I am. What can you tell us about it?

NELL

Yes, what's it about?

SUSIE

Yeah, Uncle Elliot.

ELLIOT

I don't really feel comfortable talking about it.

NELL

Oh, okay.

ELLIOT

Playwrights shouldn't discuss their work. It's so . . . *reductive.*
The work should speak for itself.

WALTER

You've written *how* many plays?

ELLIOT

One.

WALTER

Uh-huh. Have you *heard* this one yet?

ELLIOT

Actually, I'm thinking of having a reading while I'm up here.

ANNA

Good idea. With whom?

ELLIOT

Well, I was thinking all of *you.*

ANNA

Oh!

ELLIOT

I got some excellent feedback on the first act . . .

WALTER

Oh, yeah?

67

ELLIOT

People who were really blown away by it.

WALTER

Who?

(A beat.)

ELLIOT

What?

WALTER

Who was blown away by it?

ELLIOT

Knowledgeable people. Who read a lotta lotta scripts.

WALTER

Who, exactly?

ELLIOT

This guy at my agency for one. Very smart kid. Reads a ton of scripts. Really knows his stuff.

WALTER

An intern?

(A beat.)

ELLIOT

So? *(To Susie)* Went to Yale, actually. Ethan somebody?

SUSIE

(Shrugs) They're all named Ethan.

MICHAEL

(Changing the subject) So: Nell. How did you meet Walter?

NELL

(To Walter) Can I tell them?

WALTER

I have nothing to hide.

NELL

We met at Starbucks.

SUSIE

Eew, you're kidding.

NELL

I know.

ELLIOT

Didn't see *that* coming.

WALTER

I'd just finished auditions for the picture I'm about to do . . .

ELLIOT

You mean people actually audition for those things?

(Walter gives him a look before continuing.)

WALTER

And there, sitting at a table outside, was this . . . angel, crying into her latte.

ANNA

Oh, dear.

69

NELL

Soy latte.

MICHAEL

Why were you crying?

NELL

Let's just say I was having a bad day.

MICHAEL

What happened?

NELL

It's too trivial to go into. Actor stuff: I was up for a pilot; I didn't get it. I *told* you it was trivial.

MICHAEL

What was it?

NELL

Some police-procedural thing I didn't even *want*—that's the thing, I didn't even *want* it and it *still* felt like the end of the world. And I started sobbing big, existential tears. People looked at me like I was crazy, mothers moved their children away.

Then this lovely, compassionate man offered me a napkin and sat down and asked what was wrong, and we talked, for hours, till the sun went down, and he told me about the terrible loss *he* was going through, that his *family* was going through, which was a gift, really, because it certainly put *my* ridiculous crisis into perspective—and it was only then that I realized who this wonderful man was.

WALTER

What can I say? I was enchanted.

(They kiss.)

ANNA

(Put off by the kiss; to Susie, signaling) Shall we . . . ?

SUSIE

Okay, I made a gigunda salad for me and Michael and anybody else who abhors the murder of animals.

ANNA

And on that note: Dinner is served!

(They file into the dining room, Michael walks beside Nell.)

MICHAEL

(To Nell) I want to hear more about your existential crisis.

NELL

(Amused) Why? It's not terribly interesting.

MICHAEL

Oh, I don't know about *that* . . .

(Anna slips her arm through Michael's.)

ANNA

(To Michael) You sit by me.

(They exit; Elliot and Susie linger as Walter goes.)

ELLIOT

So, Walter: This new picture of yours. What is it? *Truck Stop 3?*

WALTER

Truck Stop 4, actually. There's already *been* a *Truck Stop 3*.

ELLIOT

Oh, of course. How could I forget? They're so distinct from one
another.

(Walter shakes his head and exits.)

SUSIE

(Enjoying her uncle's sarcasm) You are so bad.

ELLIOT

Can't you just see it, twenty years from now? "Walter, what're
you working on?" *(Imitating a doddering Walter as they start
to join the others) "Truck Stop 19: Attack of the Long-Haul Living
Dead!* Where these tractor trailers—a whole fucking caravan
of 'em, loaded with nuclear bombs and toxic chemicals!—are
making these hairpin turns in the Rockies! And all of a sudden, this big honking alien-zombie mothership crashes into
the mountain . . ."

(Makes an exploding sound as they exit.)

Act Two

SCENE 1

A few days later. Morning. Nell, in running clothes, comes downstairs and stretches before a run. Michael emerges from the kitchen with a thermos of coffee, surprising her.

MICHAEL

Didn't meant to sneak up on you.

NELL

I thought you'd left for the day.

MICHAEL

I'm about to. I just made a fresh pot . . .

NELL

No, thanks. I can't drink coffee before a run.

MICHAEL

(Nods, then) Don't mind me . . . *(Meaning: continue warming up)*

NELL

I'm good.

(A beat. She puts on her running shoes.)

Today's your first day on *The Guardsman*.

MICHAEL

Yup.

NELL

Excited?

MICHAEL

Yeah, I am, actually. I still get that first-day-of-school feeling, whenever I start anything.

NELL

That's refreshing. Means you aren't jaded.

MICHAEL

Not about *acting*, anyway.

NELL

I envy you. This business has done nasty things to me, things I'm not terribly proud of.

MICHAEL

How so?

> NELL

I'm constantly looking over my shoulder to see who's the new "me" coming up behind me. And resenting them. And wishing them ill. I used to be a much nicer person.

> MICHAEL

I think you're a *very* nice person.

> NELL

What makes you think *that*?

> MICHAEL

(Shrugs) Just a hunch.

(Pause.)

So, I understand congratulations are in order.

> NELL

What do you mean?

> MICHAEL

Aren't you and Walter getting / married?

> NELL

Oh! Yes. How did you know?

> MICHAEL

Elliot.

> NELL

We are. Susie doesn't know yet; Walter hasn't found a good time to tell her.

> MICHAEL

(Nods, then) Walter is a lucky man. First Kathy. Now you.

75

NELL

I'm the lucky one.

(A beat.)

You know? I'm not a mystical *woo-woo* sort of person but we were fated to meet that day; I really believe that. We rescued each other. The love he had for Kathy! I found it incredibly poignant.

MICHAEL

Poignant? Is that what you look for in a lover? Poignancy?

(She smiles, shakes her head.)

What.

NELL

You really think I'm so weak?

MICHAEL

What?

NELL

So susceptible to your irresistible charm?

(Pause.)

MICHAEL

As a matter of fact . . . I don't think that at all.

(Long pause.)

NELL

Well . . . Have a great first day.

MICHAEL

Thanks. Enjoy your run.

NELL

Will I see you later?

MICHAEL

Oh, I'll be here.

(Nell nods and goes. Michael puts his script and stuff into a small knapsack and he, too, exits.
Time shift: Later that morning. Anna enters with a tray of iced tea, followed by Susie, who reads from a copy of Mrs. Warren's Profession.*)*

ANNA

(With English accent) "Don't you be led astray by people who don't know the world, my girl. The only way for a woman to provide for herself decently is for her to be good to some man that can afford to be good to *her*."

(A slight hesitation.)

SUSIE

(Prompting) "Ask any—"

ANNA

I know! I was acting! . . .

SUSIE

Sorry.

ANNA

. . . If I need a line, I'll call for it, okay?

SUSIE

Yes, Gran, sorry.

ANNA

"Ask any lady in London society that has daughters; and she'll tell you the same, except that I tell you straight and she'll tell you crooked. That's all the difference."

SUSIE

(English accent) "My dear mother: You are a wonderful woman, you are stronger than all England. And are you really and truly not one wee bit doubtful—or—or ashamed?"

ANNA

"Well, of course, dearie, it's only good manners to be ashamed of it: it's expected from a woman. Women have to pretend to feel a great deal that they don't feel. Liz used to be angry with me for . . ." Line!

SUSIE

". . . plumping out / the truth about it."

ANNA

". . . plumping out the truth about it . . . plumping out the *truth* about it." Plumping, plumping, plumping. "She even said—"

SUSIE

"—*used to* say—"

ANNA

What?

SUSIE

"She *used to* say—"

ANNA

"—used to say"—shit!—"that when every woman could learn enough from what was going on in the world before her eyes, there was no need to mention it—"

SUSIE

(Parsing it out) "—no—need—TO—TALK—ABOUT—IT— / to—her."

ANNA

You don't have to shout! / I may be old but I'm not deaf!

SUSIE

Sorry. I'm sorry.

ANNA

Where was I?

SUSIE

"Plumping out / the truth about it."

ANNA

After that.

SUSIE

"She *used / to* say . . ."

ANNA

(Quickly, to catch up) "She-used-to-say-that-when-every-woman-could-learn-enough-from-what-was-going-on-in-the-world-before-her-eyes,-there-was-no-need-to-mention-it-"

SUSIE

"—TO—TALK— / ABOUT—IT—"

ANNA

Fuck! Give me that.

(She snatches away the script.)

I'm not ready to run this.

(Anna sits on the couch and looks over the script. Pause.)

SUSIE

I can't believe Michael left this morning without saying good-bye.

ANNA

He didn't leave. It's his first day of rehearsal.

SUSIE

You mean he's staying here *again*?

ANNA

Yes.

SUSIE

I thought he was supposed to spend a night or two.

ANNA

He was.

SUSIE

It's already been *four*. Isn't his house aired-out yet?

ANNA

Apparently not to his liking. Are you going to let me study?

SUSIE

Sorry.

(Susie watches Anna concentrate on the script. Silence.)

Do you realize this is the quietest it's been here for days?

ANNA

Shhh.

(Susie gets a photo album and begins to leaf through it, distracting Anna.)

I don't know how you can look at that. If I see a picture of her somewhere, I have to turn away, quickly, before my brain can tell me whose face I'm looking at.

I go through each day trying not to think about her, but I have lapses, I do, I forget she's gone, and want to tell her something, and have to remind myself: Oh, that's right . . .

So I play this game with myself. You know what I do?

(Susie shakes her head.)

I imagine she's working, off on location, shooting a movie.

SUSIE

Where?

ANNA

Someplace magical and far away. One of those remote islands in the Pacific with white-sand beaches and turquoise water; and cloudless, sky blue skies. And this little island is so off-the-grid, she can't contact us; as much as she'd like to, she can't. But it's all right because she's having such a marvelous time.

SUSIE

(Smiling) Mm.

(Nell returns, sweaty and breathless, from her run.)

NELL

Phew, it's getting humid out there!

(Nell sees Susie return the photo album to the shelf.)

Oh, I'm sorry, am I interrupting something?

ANNA

You've rescued me from learning my lines.

NELL

Have you seen Walter?

ANNA

(Refers to the patio) Out there. Reading. Hasn't budged.

NELL

(Sees Walter asleep outside) He's sleeping. Poor baby. His knee kept him up all night.

(Susie walks past Nell.)

Don't go. Not on my account.

SUSIE

I've got stuff to do anyway.

NELL

Susie . . .

SUSIE

Only my family gets to call me Susie.

(Susie is gone.)

NELL

I can't seem to say the right thing.

ANNA

Give her time. It's a lot all at once.

(Nell nods, serves herself iced tea. She sees the Shaw script.)

NELL

So. *Mrs. Warren's Profession.*

ANNA

Uh-huh.

NELL

I did *Pygmalion* in acting school.

ANNA

Oh? Where was that?

NELL

DePaul? In Chicago?

ANNA

I know where DePaul is.

NELL

Some people don't.

(A beat.)

You know? *You* have the career I used to dream about.

ANNA

I do?

NELL

Yes. The way you go from stage to film and back to stage again
. . . You're a Broadway star!

ANNA

There are no Broadway stars, dear. Not anymore. Oh, there *are*
stars on Broadway but they're not *Broadway* stars. In the old
days, every season there'd be the new Gerry Page play, or the
new Julie Harris. *They* were Broadway stars. Those days are
over. I was born in the wrong era, I'm afraid.

NELL

Why do you say that?

ANNA

I can't get something on.

NELL

I can't believe that.

ANNA

My TVQ isn't high enough, my agents tell me. "Do more TV."
If I did a series like our friend, Michael . . .

WALTER

(Entering from the patio) Do it.

ANNA

Hello, Walter.

NELL

Hi.

WALTER

Hello, my darling.

NELL

How're you feeling?

WALTER

Old.

ANNA

Join the club.

NELL

How's the knee?

WALTER

Better. I'm gonna have to get the damn thing replaced, no getting around it. I can't tell you how much I'm looking forward to being on set with a bum knee.

NELL

Anna was just saying how she can't get a play on Broadway. I can't believe that.

WALTER

I can.

ANNA

There are no real producers anymore. People with vision. And balls.

WALTER

You can't blame the producers.

ANNA

Why can't I?

WALTER

They have to sell tickets. Can't have them losing their shirts. Then there'd be *no* plays on Broadway.

ANNA

You're quite right, Walter. Why don't you send me out to sea on a fiery barge? Now. Before I'm even dead.

WALTER

I wouldn't dream of doing that.

ANNA

I'm a throwback. Isn't that awful? To live long enough to be a throwback? A leading lady without a stage. My audience—the matinee ladies and their poor husbands—is dead or dying or going deaf. And I fear I'm not far behind.

NELL

No, you look fantastic.

WALTER

You do!

ANNA

You mean for my age.

NELL

I mean for any age.

ANNA

I've done a little sprucing up, I admit, a little spackling and sanding here and there.

NELL

Well, *I'm* your audience, too, and I'd love to see you do just about anything.

ANNA

Why, thank you, dear.

NELL

Would you excuse me? I'm pretty grungy, I've got to take a shower.

(Nell kisses Walter; Anna averts her eyes.)

WALTER

Bye, darlin'.

(Nell goes upstairs. Pause.)

Thank you for hosting her. I know this can't be easy.

ANNA

She's lovely, Walter.

WALTER

Isn't she?

ANNA

I suppose you'd like my blessing.

WALTER

Of course I would.

ANNA

I have nothing against *her*. It's the *fact* of her I have trouble with.

WALTER

I know.

(Susie returns and heads to the front door.)

SUSIE

Oh. You're awake.

WALTER

Hey. Where you going?

SUSIE

I promised Gran . . .

ANNA

That can wait.

WALTER

I feel like I haven't gotten to see you since I got here.

SUSIE

Maybe that's 'cause you haven't gotten to see me since you got here.

WALTER

Whose fault is that?

(Anna gives Susie a look and goes to the kitchen so they can be alone. Susie reluctantly sits.)

Thank you.

(Pause.)

So? Tell me how you are.

SUSIE

Fine.

WALTER

How are you really?

(Susie shrugs, doesn't look at him. Pause.)

How'd your term end up?

SUSIE

Two A's, two A-minuses.

WALTER

Great, but that's not what I'm asking.

SUSIE

You pay my tuition . . . Don't you want to know if I'm wasting
your money?

WALTER

I meant . . . I know you were feeling blue.

SUSIE

Of course I was feeling blue, my mother died. I miss my mother.

WALTER

I know you do, kiddo. So do I.

SUSIE

Really?

WALTER

Of course I do. You think I want to forget your mother?

SUSIE

How could you bring her here?

WALTER

Susie.

SUSIE

How could you bring her / to this house?

WALTER

I ran it by your grandmother; she said / it was okay.

SUSIE

My grandmother? What about me? Don't I get a say?

(Pause.)

WALTER

Give Nell a chance. Let down your guard. You'll see. She's a fantastic woman. There's a lot about her that reminds me of your mother. They would have liked each other; I mean it, they would have been friends.

SUSIE

(Realizes) Oh shit. You're not going to *marry* her . . .

WALTER

Sweetie . . .

SUSIE

Really, Daddy? Are you really going to / *marry* her?

WALTER

Honey . . .

SUSIE

Mom's barely been gone a year.

WALTER

I know, the speed of all this surprised me, too.

SUSIE

Couldn't you live together? Why do you have to run and get married? She's not pregnant, is she?

WALTER

No. Your mother spoiled me: I *like* being married. I like the comfort it brings. I missed that. This was the only time I could introduce you; I know it's awkward . . .

SUSIE

You think?

WALTER

I didn't know what else to do! I go back to L.A. next week, start shooting on the fifteenth . . . You know how crazy things get . . .

SUSIE

Oh, I know.

WALTER

. . . Then you go back to school . . . and before you'd know it, we wouldn't be seeing each other again till Thanksgiving or Christmas. I didn't want all that time to go by before you got to meet her. I'm really sorry.

After we buried your mother . . . and I was all alone in that big house . . . My life felt pretty much over. Certainly my happiness. It was hard for me, too, you know.

SUSIE

I know.

WALTER

Maybe you *don't* know. The minute I saw Nell . . .

> SUSIE

You sound like a Lifetime movie.

> WALTER

We used to be able to talk, you and I. Didn't we? I'd drive you to school, way the hell out in Studio City? Sitting in traffic on the 405? We'd talk about everything! I couldn't get you to shut up!

> SUSIE

It's easy to talk to your parents when you're in the car, driving. Nobody has to look at each other.

(Walter gets an idea.)

> WALTER

Come. Let's go for a ride.

> SUSIE

No, I can't. I have to run these errands for Gran.

(She starts to go; he joins her.)

> WALTER

I'll go with you.

(She thinks about it.)

> SUSIE

On one condition.

> WALTER

What.

> SUSIE

You let me drive the Porsche.

WALTER

What?!

(She shrugs. Walter considers it.)

Oh, what the hell . . .

(Walter tosses her the keys. As he limps out with Susie:)

The clutch is very sensitive . . .

SUSIE

(Exiting) I know how to drive a stick; you taught me . . .

(Time shift: Late afternoon. A gentle rain. Elliot hurries down-stairs holding his unbound manuscript; he's packing it in a satchel when Nell, wearing a mac, enters from the patio.)

NELL

Nice rain. I love that earthy smell.

ELLIOT

I finished my play.

NELL

Congratulations.

ELLIOT

I was up all night writing. It was fantastic: I finally figured out how it should end.

NELL

Good for you.

ELLIOT

You stare at a blank page for days and all of a sudden you know just what to do.

(They look at one another for a beat.)

I'm gonna go make copies.

(He starts to go.)

NELL

Elliot.

(He stops.)

ELLIOT

Yeah?

NELL

I owe you an apology.

ELLIOT

Me?

NELL

I *should* have let you know about me and Walter.

ELLIOT

Wow. You mean we weren't "just colleagues"?

NELL

I was being disingenuous. Of *course* we were friends.

ELLIOT

(Joking) I'm feeling a little woozy; you mind if I . . .

(He stumbles to the couch and sits.)

So I'm not crazy?

NELL

I didn't say *that*. I said we were friends.

(She laughs. Pause.)

ELLIOT

Who would have thought you'd come back into my life this way?
Deus ex Walter.

NELL

I know, right?

ELLIOT

Do you ever imagine what might have happened if I'd made a
move all those years ago?

NELL

No.

ELLIOT

That might have changed everything. But, no, I was too afraid
of bursting the bubble. I couldn't risk it. Not for something as
fleeting as lust.

NELL

Enough of the hapless, hangdog routine!

ELLIOT

You think I put this on? You think I would *choose* to be this way?
It's *exhausting* being me. I wouldn't recommend it to anyone.

NELL

You know? You were *funny* when I met you. You made me laugh.

ELLIOT

You thought I was funny?

NELL

You know I did. Whenever I feel the slightest twinge of affection towards you, you . . .

ELLIOT

You feel affection?

NELL

Oh, stop it. You're your own worst enemy, you know that? I wish you would just—

(He kisses her mouth. She recoils.)

Elliot! / No!

ELLIOT

I'm sorry, I'm sorry.

(She moves to the staircase.)

Don't go.

NELL

(As she runs upstairs) Just when I thought I could have a civilized conversation with you . . . !

(A beat.)

ELLIOT

(Shouts after her) Why would you think that?

(He gets his satchel and goes out the front door.)

Scene 2

Later that night. A roiling and rumbly summer night; a thunderstorm is brewing. The company, drinks in hand, enters the living room after dinner. Michael is speaking. The others listen intently, except for Elliot.

MICHAEL

(Entering) The civil war is so insane . . . I mean, these tribes are killing each other over fishing rights! Who has the rights to fish in certain ponds! These kids have nothing. No hope. No families. They watch their fathers dragged away, never to be seen again, their mothers raped. Brutalized. Kidnapped. The rebels put guns in the boys' hands and turn them into soldiers when they're as young as six.

WALTER

Six! / My God.

MICHAEL

And the girls, well, you can imagine what happens to them.

SUSIE

Uch . . .

WALTER

So, once they're rescued from the rebels . . . ?

MICHAEL

Get 'em into schools. Problem is, there *are* no schools. They've been burned to the ground, or washed away during rainy season. So we build them.

NELL

You literally build them?

MICHAEL

Uh-huh.

NELL

With your own two hands?

MICHAEL

With my own / two hands.

ANNA

Isn't that marvelous?

ELLIOT

(To Susie) You got any weed?

SUSIE

What?! No!

MICHAEL

If we can give them a safe haven . . .

ELLIOT

(A new idea; to Susie) Ooo, where'd your mom keep her stash?

SUSIE	ANNA
(Annoyed) I don't know.	Elliot!

(Elliot looks around the room.)

MICHAEL

A safe haven where they're allowed to be kids, not soldiers or sex slaves, and teach them basic skills that might give them a shot at a living wage, they might just have a chance in hell.

NELL

Oh, Michael, that is so . . .

ANNA

(To Elliot) What are you doing?

ELLIOT

Looking for Kathy's medical marijuana. / *(To himself)* There's got to be some left.

MICHAEL

This one boy . . .

ELLIOT

Tah-dahh!

(Elliot finds a plastic bag with weed and proceeds to roll a joint.)

ANNA

Really, Elliot. Not in front of Susie.

SUSIE

Are you kidding? Far worse was done in my presence.

ANNA

At school?

SUSIE

By this family! In this house!

NELL

(To Michael) You were saying about this boy?

ANNA

Sorry, Michael.

SUSIE	WALTER
(To Michael) Sorry.	Please. Go on.

NELL

Tell us about that boy. Please.

MICHAEL

He wouldn't speak, or make eye contact. But I sat with him, a few minutes every day I was there, and talked about baseball, soccer, whatever I could think of, and had no idea if anything was getting through to him.

On my last day, I was saying my good-byes, he came up to me—

(He chokes up.)

I'll never forget this. He looked up at me—really *looked* at me, for the first time—and held out this piece of paper . . . *(To Nell)* He was giving me a present. Something to remember him by. He . . .

(He's moved. Nell is, too, and spontaneously touches his hand, which doesn't go unnoticed by Anna.)

NELL

(Gently) Go on.

MICHAEL

He made a drawing. Of the two of us. I still have it.

(He and Nell share a moment.)

ELLIOT

(Takes a hit of the joint; derisively) Oh, brother.

ANNA

Can I get anyone more wine?

(Nell removes her hand from Michael's.)

WALTER

How much does a school like that cost?

MICHAEL

Twenty-five thousand.

WALTER

Where do I send a check?

MICHAEL

Oh, I'll get you the info, / don't worry.

WALTER

I'm serious.

MICHAEL

Hey, man, so am I!

ANNA

Bravo, Michael! What a godsend you are!

MICHAEL

No, no. There are people who devote their *lives* to this stuff. I'm just there to help shine a light on it.

ANNA

(Genuinely) Aw . . .

WALTER

We send our checks and buy our tables at fundraisers, but you actually go there . . .

101

NELL

It's true.

ANNA

If more people were like Michael, we . . .

(The others agree.)

ELLIOT

(Loudly, above the murmurs) Jesus! You sound like a fucking public service announcement!

SUSIE	ANNA
Uncle Elliot . . .	Elliot. Really. Must you?

ELLIOT

Spare me the self-congratulation.

NELL

That isn't fair.

ANNA

(To Michael) Don't pay attention to him, he's jealous.

ELLIOT

It's all about you! Saint Michael of the Congo!

MICHAEL

It's not about *me* at all! You don't get it! I *lose* myself in this work. That's what I love about it.

ELLIOT

You go to the Congo the same reason you come to Williamstown: To feel better about yourself.

WALTER

Jesus, Elliot . . .

MICHAEL

(Overlapping) Oh, is that what it's about? Feeling better about myself? I feel better knowing I've done something for the greater good, so yeah.

NELL

(To Elliot) What's the alternative? To do nothing? Like you? I'm not saying I'm any better but Michael is actually doing some good in the world.

SUSIE

Yeah.

MICHAEL

(To Nell) Thank you.

ELLIOT

Of course you think that, that's what he wants you to think!

ANNA

(To Elliot) Put. That. Away.

ELLIOT

Anybody want some . . . ?

(He offers the joint to Susie, who swats him away.)

MICHAEL

I'll take a hit of that.

(Elliot passes the joint.)

SUSIE

(Admonishing) Michael . . . !

MICHAEL

What.

(He takes a hit.)

ELLIOT

You and your rich and famous friends . . . you pick your pet causes / but it's . . .

MICHAEL

Cut me some slack, man. I figured, if I'm going to be a celebrity or whatever the hell you want to call what I am— *(To Nell)* I used to be an actor, now I'm a celebrity—then I'm going to put it to good use. / Y'know?

ANNA

Hear, hear.

MICHAEL

I refuse to be a prisoner in my own house, behind gates and security cameras. I don't want to live like that. I want to be out in the world and *do* something. Something that matters. What else am I gonna do? Stay home and party all the time? Fuck around, put shit up my nose? I tried all that; believe me.

SUSIE

You did?

MICHAEL

Lost a good year, year-and-a-half of my life to it.

NELL

(To Michael) What happened?

MICHAEL

It's not worth going into.

(Rumbles of thunder. Lights brown-out then restore. "Ooo's.")

WALTER

It's definitely trying to do something / out there.

(Elliot stands and clinks his glass to get their attention.)

MICHAEL

(To Elliot) Yes . . . ?

ELLIOT

May I have your attention, please?

(Elliot continues clinking after everyone is quiet.)

MICHAEL

Yes?!

ELLIOT

I suppose you're wondering why I called you all here today . . .
Our father, Art—I mean, Leonard—who art in heaven / or wher-
ever the hell he ended up . . .

ANNA

(To Susie) What is he doing?

ELLIOT

It's a good thing Dad didn't live to bury his only daughter; it
would've killed him. Bu-du-bum. But seriously folks . . .

(Susie gently tries to rein him in.)

SUSIE

Why don't we go upstairs?

ELLIOT

I don't want to go upstairs.

(Susie reaches for his glass, which he brusquely pulls away. More rumbles. Storm approaching.)

NELL

(To Michael) Front's coming through.

ELLIOT

Lest we forget why we're here . . . I'd like to propose a toast. To the missing woman. The woman who is missed. Conspicuous in her absence. To Kathy. One year gone. But not forgotten.

(The others raise their glasses in an awkward toast.)

THE OTHERS

(Not in unison) To Kathy!

(A loud crack of thunder, followed by a flash of lightning and a torrential downpour.)

WALTER

Here it comes!

ANNA

It's raining in! Close the doors!

(Susie closes them.)

MICHAEL

Wow, it's really coming down!

NELL

I love storms like this!

(The lights flicker, then go out entirely. A collective gasp. Ad-libbed pandemonium in the dark:)

WALTER	ANNA
Oh, shit!	Oh, no!

ELLIOT

Ah ha! Kathy's revenge!
Where have we got flashlights?

ANNA

I don't remember.

ELLIOT

You don't remember?!

ANNA

Check the kitchen drawer that has everything.

SUSIE

The hurricane lamps!

ANNA

Oh, damn, I left windows open upstairs.

MICHAEL

I'll go.

(Michael goes upstairs by the light of his iPhone, followed by Anna.

Vignettes play in light provided only by flashlight, hurricane lamp, iPhone or candle. Time is contiguous; we shift minutes, sometimes seconds between scenes. Steady rain. Rumbles and flashes of lightning.

Walter and Nell snuggle in a chair by hurricane-lamp light.)

WALTER

Elliot's in rare form tonight.

NELL

It's all right. I can handle Elliot.

WALTER

I shouldn't have brought you here. It was selfish.

NELL

No . . .

WALTER

I had to be here. For Susie.

NELL

Of course you did.

WALTER

How are you holding up?

NELL

Okay. I feel a little like Joan Fontaine in *Rebecca*, but aside from that . . .

WALTER

Am I a terrible man?

NELL

Yes, you're awful.

(She kisses him; their kissing progresses. More thunder.)

WALTER

(Remembers) Oh, shit!

NELL

What.

WALTER

I left the top down on the Porsche!

(He hobbles off, cursing his pain.)

NELL

Walter! Wait!

(Nell goes after him.
Time shift: Michael enters, followed by Elliot. Michael begins
to get ready for bed. Elliot dons a windbreaker.)

MICHAEL

Why must you be so fucking cynical?

ELLIOT

Earnest, holier-than-thou bullshit does that to me. You're not
running for student council president, / for crissake!

MICHAEL

What the fuck does that even mean?

ELLIOT

You don't need to play up the activism to impress girls.

MICHAEL

I'm not "playing up" anything.

ELLIOT

If this is what helps you get laid . . .

MICHAEL

Whoa! First of all, this may come as a shock to you but I need very little help getting laid, thank you. And, secondly, I certainly don't need to exploit women's sympathy to do it. When did you get to be such an asshole?

ELLIOT

(Shrugs) I've always been kind of an asshole. I mean, really, when you think about it.

MICHAEL

Y'know? You may be onto something there . . .

(Elliot starts to go.)

Where are you going?

ELLIOT

I'm gonna do a little gardening.

MICHAEL

Elliot! . . .

(Elliot exits to the garden with his flashlight.
Michael gets bedding from a trunk and prepares to make up the couch. Susie, in a nightshirt, comes downstairs by the light of a hurricane lamp.)

SUSIE

Want help?

MICHAEL

Sure.

SUSIE

I wish you didn't get stoned with him.

MICHAEL

What? I had one hit!

SUSIE

Don't encourage him. In any way. Please? His drinking is bad enough but he shouldn't be self-medicating, especially not while he's taking antidepressants.

MICHAEL

He's taking antidepressants?

SUSIE

Isn't everybody? Well, they don't seem to be working. For him, I mean. Me, I swear by them.

My mother made him promise, on her deathbed, he would clean up his act but he hasn't even tried.

MICHAEL

I'm sorry; I didn't know it had gotten so bad. Your grandmother hadn't said anything.

SUSIE

Of course not. She's in denial about everything. Will you promise not to encourage him?

MICHAEL

Yes I won't encourage him.

SUSIE

Please, Michael, / I mean it.

MICHAEL

I said yes! You worry too much, you know that? It's not healthy for a person as young as you to worry so much.

SUSIE

I worry about everyone. That's what I do.
What did you mean before about your lost year?

MICHAEL

(Shrugs) That's what it was. Typical Hollywood insanity. My
first taste of success, I went a little crazy. Thankfully, I realized
I was going crazy and did something about it.

SUSIE

And you've been okay?

MICHAEL

Reasonably, yeah.

SUSIE

If you ever find yourself there again . . . Will you let me know?

MICHAEL

If I ever do? Yeah. Yeah, I will.

SUSIE

Good.

(Pause.)

MICHAEL

I can do the rest, I'm keeping you up.

SUSIE

I don't care.

MICHAEL

We should get to sleep. We've got Elliot's reading in the morning.

SUSIE

Yeah. Okay. Good night.

MICHAEL

Good night.

(She starts to go but stops.)

What is it?

SUSIE

(With difficulty) The last few nights? Having you here? Sleeping under the same roof? Knowing you're *right there* . . . In the flesh. Breathing. It's almost too much. I mean . . . I've thought about you . . . that way . . . from the first time I started thinking those things.

MICHAEL

Susie . . .

SUSIE

That's a little girl's name. I'm not a little girl anymore.

MICHAEL

Sweetie, you should go to bed.

(She lingers for a moment before disappearing into the darkness.)

(To himself) Oh, boy . . .

(Time shift: Michael takes off his jeans, sets them down on a chair. Anna comes downstairs holding a candle, a pillow tucked under her arm.)

ANNA

(Like a hotel maid) "Housekeeping."

MICHAEL

Hi.

ANNA

I thought maybe you could try a different pillow tonight. This one *(Meaning: the one he's been using)* has lost so many of its feathers . . .

MICHAEL

I hadn't noticed.

ANNA

You've really been okay down here? I feel like such a bad hostess.

MICHAEL

It's been fine, really.

(She puts her hand on his chest.)

ANNA

Great to have you here, Michael.

MICHAEL

Great to be here.

(She touches his cheek.)

ANNA

It's a comfort to me. Really.

MICHAEL

I'm glad.

(Pause. She moves a step closer, he moves a step away.)

ANNA

Well . . . Good night.

MICHAEL

Good night.

(Anna snatches the pillow she had delivered as she heads back upstairs. He raises an eyebrow.

*Time shift: Michael, stretched out on the couch, is illuminated by his iPhone. Nell comes downstairs by the light of her iPhone, sees him.)**

NELL

Oh.

MICHAEL

Hey.

NELL

Sorry. I just . . .

MICHAEL

That's okay.

NELL

I didn't mean to disturb you.

MICHAEL

You're not disturbing me.

NELL

I wanted a glass of water.

MICHAEL

Help yourself.

(As she goes to the kitchen:)

Could I have one, too?

115

NELL

(Off) Sure.

(She returns with two glasses of water, hands him one.)

Thanks.

(They both drink.)

Well . . . Good night.

(She starts to go.)

MICHAEL

Sorry if I went on before.

NELL

(Stops) What?

MICHAEL

About Congo.

NELL

Not at all. I found it inspiring.

MICHAEL

I can't help it; once I get started . . .

NELL

If I had something like that in my life . . . that really mattered
. . . I'd want to share it with people, too.

MICHAEL

I didn't want to make you feel bad . . .

NELL

You didn't. You just got me thinking. We get so caught up in our own little dramas . . . we forget that we share the planet with people whose lives are truly hellish. It's good to be reminded that we *can* make a difference. Even if it's convincing *one* boy that someone in the world cares what happens to him.

MICHAEL

That boy did more for me than I could have possibly done for him. To him, I wasn't famous, I was just a man who showed him kindness.

NELL

Didn't you want to be famous?

MICHAEL

Are you kidding? I wanted it so badly . . . I can't remember *why* it was so important to me but it was. Then . . . one morning, you wake up, on one of those glorious L.A. mornings, with someone beside you you don't love, in a house you once dreamt about, only now it's *your* house but it doesn't *feel* like your house and probably never will. And you drive to the studio in your super energy-efficient car, and memorize pages of inane dialogue for which you're paid a *stupid* amount of money and . . . You do that enough mornings . . . You begin to wonder . . .

NELL

. . . if that's what you really wanted.

MICHAEL

That's right.

NELL

I understand.

MICHAEL

I think you do.

(They look at each other in sexually charged silence.)

NELL

I should go up.

MICHAEL

Stay. Talk.

NELL

Walter will wonder where I went.

MICHAEL

Walter is zonked out on Vicodin.

(She starts to go. He stands and takes her hand, stopping her.)

Stay.

(They look at one another. He steps closer when suddenly, power is restored! The lights go on—revealing Elliot, flowers in hand; Anna and Susie, who have been eavesdropping from the shadows, unseen by one another.)

ELLIOT

Oops.

(He chucks the flowers and leaves.
Abashed, the women go their separate ways, leaving Michael alone.
Intermission.)

Act Three

Scene 1

The following morning.
   Michael is unmaking his bed. Susie warily comes downstairs
and helps him.

MICHAEL

Morning.

(Silence.)

SUSIE

What were you thinking?

MICHAEL

I *wasn't* thinking.

SUSIE

Not with your *brain*, anyway.

MICHAEL

I'm sorry you all had to see that.

SUSIE

I'll bet you are. I'll bet *she* is, too.

MICHAEL

Nell did nothing wrong. I asked her for a glass of water . . .

SUSIE

Uh-huh.

MICHAEL

Look, whatever it *appeared* to be, it was my fault; I take full responsibility. Please don't punish *her* for it; she's a good person.

SUSIE

What about you? Are you in the habit of hitting on other men's fiancées?

MICHAEL

I'm really not. I don't want you to get the wrong idea.

SUSIE

Too late.

(Elliot comes downstairs carrying his scripts, sees Michael.)

ELLIOT

Is it safe?

(Michael feels the chill but doesn't respond.)

(To Susie) Could you make sure your grandmother's up?

SUSIE

Okay.

ELLIOT

Thanks.

(Susie goes back upstairs. Michael takes out his bag, starting to pack.)

Where do you think *you're* going?

MICHAEL

I thought it would be best if I, uh . . .

ELLIOT

Un-uh. Not so fast, Romeo. I need you for my reading.

MICHAEL

Don't you think maybe we should do it some other time?

ELLIOT

Oh, we're doing it. You promised. We arranged it around *your* fucking schedule.

(Elliot hands Michael a script.)

You're the lead. Congratulations.

(Walter enters from the kitchen with a tray of coffee mugs and a carafe.)

WALTER

(Brightly) Show time! Boy, I'm really looking forward to hearing this play!

ELLIOT

Where's Nell?

WALTER

I'll get her.

(Anna and Susie come downstairs.)

ANNA

Tell me again: *Why* are we doing this so unconscionably early?

SUSIE

Michael has rehearsal.

ANNA

Oh, that's right.

WALTER

Good morning!

(Walter hands Anna a cup of coffee.)

ANNA

Thank you, darling. I don't know about *you* but I slept miserably last night.

WALTER

Not me. I slept like a baby. *(Calls)* Nell, honey? Are you coming?

ANNA

What about you, Michael? How did *you* sleep?

MICHAEL

Not very well.

ANNA

Oh, what a shame.

.

WALTER

(Calls) Nell? Here she comes.

(Nell sheepishly comes downstairs, all eyes on her.)

NELL

Sorry.

(Walter kisses her cheek. Elliot distributes scripts.)

ELLIOT

I highlighted everybody's lines.

ANNA

How thoughtful.

(Elliot offers Nell a script, teases her by withholding it before handing it over. She takes a seat.)

WALTER

All right, let's get this show on the road, shall we?

ANNA

Yes, let's.

ELLIOT

Okay. I'll read stage directions. Ready?

WALTER

Ready.

(They open their scripts.)

ELLIOT

(Reads) *"The Descent of Man."* Working title. "A new play by
Elliot Cooper." *(They turn the page)* "Act One. Scene 1. Lights
up: A house in the country. A forty-year-old man addresses the
audience."

(He gestures to Michael to begin.
Curtain.
The curtain rises on the scene about two hours later. Except
for Elliot, the company's body language suggests that annoy-
ance and boredom have set in.)

(Reads) ". . . and the curtain falls. End of play."

(He closes the script. Pause.)

MICHAEL

That's it?

ELLIOT

Yeah. That's what "end of play" means.

ANNA

Well! That was . . .

WALTER

Yes! Bravo!

(Walter claps. The others join in, tepidly.)

NELL

Congratulations.

ELLIOT

Thanks.

124

MICHAEL

(To Elliot) Wait. He kills himself?

ELLIOT

Uh-huh.

SUSIE

Excuse me, I have to go pee.

NELL

Me, too.

(Susie goes to the upstairs bathroom; Nell to the one on the first floor.)

MICHAEL

So . . . at the end . . . The mother is dead; he's killed her.

ELLIOT

Right.

ANNA

I'm parched. *(To Walter)* Would you like some water?

WALTER

Yes, please.

(She goes.)

MICHAEL

He's taken pills and the house is engulfed in flames. Burning rafters falling all around them.

ELLIOT

Yeah . . .

WALTER

How are you going to pull that off on *stage*?

ELLIOT

What.

MICHAEL

That was *my* question.

WALTER

Burning down the house. I mean, it's a great image . . . In a movie you can do that and it'll look spectacular. On stage, though . . .

ELLIOT

I know the difference between stage and film, Walter, I don't know, some designer'll figure it out. They love that stuff.

WALTER

What happens to it now?

ELLIOT

I try to get it produced.

MICHAEL

Where you gonna take it?

ELLIOT

I don't know. Walter, where would *you* take it?

WALTER

I have no idea.

ELLIOT

Think. You must have *some* / idea . . .

WALTER

I wouldn't know who to approach.

ELLIOT

Oh, come on, you know everybody and everybody certainly knows you . . .

WALTER

Not really; not anymore. I'm out of touch with the theater scene; I haven't done a play in years. It's a whole new generation. These kids don't know who I am. Or was.

(Anna returns with her and Walter's water.)

Your *mother* would be a much more reliable source.

(Anna glares at Walter.)

ELLIOT

Mother?

ANNA

You *are* going to do some more work on it first, though, right?

ELLIOT

Yeah . . .

ANNA

Aren't you?

ELLIOT

Why, you didn't like it?

ANNA

I didn't say that. I assume you'll want to do more work on it before you start sending it out.

127

ELLIOT

You didn't like it.

ANNA

Elliot, it's your first draft of your first play! You can't write one play—the first draft of a single play—and expect it to work right off the bat.

ELLIOT

So you're saying it doesn't work?

ANNA

All I'm saying is, darling, writing plays is a very difficult pursuit.

ELLIOT

Really? I had no idea.

ANNA

Just because someone writes a play doesn't make them a playwright.

ELLIOT

Wow.

WALTER

She's right, champ.

ANNA

I think it's marvelous you found yourself a, a hobby.

ELLIOT

A hobby?!

ANNA

Something that really gives you pleasure.

ELLIOT

This isn't a hobby, Mother. It's a calling.

ANNA

Being a playwright, darling? A *play*wright? Acting isn't demoralizing enough, you choose *play*writing?

ELLIOT

The nerve of me! The arrogance! . . .

ANNA

(To Walter) Help me out here.

WALTER

Go ahead. You're doing fine.

ELLIOT

(Continuous) . . . That *I*—a talentless schmuck like me!—

ANNA	MICHAEL
Oh, God . . .	Elliot!

ELLIOT

(Continuous) —might have something illuminating to say about the human condition . . .

(Anna emits a scoffing sound.)

Are you laughing?!

ANNA

No.

ELLIOT

You think that's funny?

129

ANNA

I don't think it's funny, no.

ELLIOT

That's right: Writing plays is off-limits to someone like me. Only a chosen few have the right. What am I but a mere interloper?

ANNA

Oh, darling, why is it so important for you to be an artist?

ELLIOT

Why? Because artistic accomplishment is the only way to feel anything resembling *love* around here!

MICHAEL

Calm. The fuck. Down.

ELLIOT

Fuck you, Michael. *You're* one to talk about self-control!

(Michael throws his hands up and exits to the patio.)

(Continuous, to Anna) Why can't you be supportive / for a change?

ANNA

I *am* being supportive.

ELLIOT

No, you're not.

ANNA

Darling, if you announced that you wanted to become a . . . I don't know, a massage therapist or a . . .

ELLIOT

Massage therapist?

ANNA

. . . a high school *English* teacher. Bravo! What a noble profession. But deciding at your age that—poof!—you're a playwright?! It's magical thinking, darling, / it really is.

ELLIOT

You think if you throw in a "dear" or a "darling" it mitigates every hateful, demeaning thing you say to me, / don't you.

ANNA

Do you think it's easy telling your child the truth? Do you? Shall I pretend your play was a work of genius? Is that what you want? Lies? I can lie; I pretend for a living. Marvelous! Absolutely brilliant! All it was, was a childish attempt to get back at me! / To embarrass me!

ELLIOT

That's right, it's all about you!

ANNA

You insist on turning me into this . . . gorgon, this monstrous mother. You take pleasure in it. What a sick exercise: I can't believe I was a party just now to my own vilification. *(To Walter)* How does he do it? *He* behaves abominably and *I'm* the one who ends up feeling guilty!

(She exits. Silence.)

ELLIOT

You've been awfully quiet, Walter.

WALTER

You're not interested in what I / have to say.

131

ELLIOT

That's not true, I'm *very* interested. I want your feedback.

WALTER

Artists *say* they want feedback but the fact is: They don't, not really, all they want is praise. I've lived long enough to know . . . People who beg for your opinion—not just about art, about anything—what they *really* want is validation of the choices they've already made. Someone'll ask, "Which color do you think I should paint my living room? The blue or the green?" "I like the green." "Well, I'm going with the blue." What's the point in my saying *anything*? It won't matter one way or another because you've already made up your mind. And that's fine. But don't act like you give a shit what I have to say.

ELLIOT

Yeah, well, you're wrong: I do care.

WALTER

You do, huh.

ELLIOT

Yes.

WALTER

What is it about you, Elliot, this gift you have for self-mortification? You practically insist that people hurt you. All right, I can do that. You want to know what I thought of your play?

ELLIOT

Yes.

WALTER

I thought it was appalling. Okay? Amateur. Masturbatory. Shall I go on? For our friendship's sake, please, let's just drop it.

ELLIOT

Friendship? What friendship? We're not friends, Walter. We *were* in-laws. Now that Kathy's gone, are you *any*thing to me anymore? Except an irritant? A pebble in my shoe? In all the time we've known each other—that you've been part of this family—have you ever, once, used me in anything?

WALTER

Oh, Jesus . . .

ELLIOT

Have you?

WALTER

. . . What is this: "What have you done for me lately?"

ELLIOT

What have you done for me—ever. Some dipshitty little part. A walk-on. / Anything.

WALTER

You know my policy: I never work with family.

ELLIOT

That didn't stop you from working with Kathy . . .

WALTER

She was my wife.

ELLIOT

I hate to tell you but your wife is your family. And what about Mother? How many times have you worked with Mother?

WALTER

Your mother is one of the all-time greats. Of course I'm going to work with her.

ELLIOT

So what am I to you? Huh? Just another schmuck actor?

WALTER

You need to pull yourself together, champ.

(Walter gently touches Elliot's shoulder; Elliot brusquely pulls away.)

ELLIOT

You need to fuck off . . . Champ.

(Pause.)

WALTER

You think coming in to audition is hard? Try sitting on the other side of the table for a change. Actors I've known for thirty, forty years—people I started out with, people I admired—schlep in to read. Angry. Desperate. Cracking too many jokes, laughing too hard. Pushing it. You smell flop sweat the way a dog smells fear. It's *awful* seeing people you care about so exposed, just horrible.

I've sat there when *you've* come in, Elliot. Failure and aggression follow you into the room. Like a storm cloud. With this Fuck-you, I-don't-need-you chip on your shoulder. The vibe you give off . . . You don't *want* the job.

ELLIOT

Is that right.

WALTER

You think you *should* want it; you go through the motions. But you don't. Not really.

ELLIOT

And why is that?

WALTER

Because if you got the job you'd have to deliver, and you're terrified that you won't be able to do it. You'd bomb out. Or, worse, you couldn't cut it and I'd have to fire you. No one wants to work with you, Elliot. You've done a very good job of making yourself radioactive. You're on everyone's life-is-too-short list.

(Pause.)

ELLIOT

I idolized you, Walter. You know that?

WALTER

Elliot, please.

ELLIOT

When Kathy first brought you around? . . . I thought: "Wow: Walter Keegan, the famous director: How cool is that?" And to be an intimate of yours?—your brother-in-law?! I felt so damn proud. And then . . . When you started making shlock . . .

WALTER

Okay, here we go.

ELLIOT

. . . First that scatological teen comedy . . .

WALTER

Coming-of-age story.

ELLIOT

You wish. And when you stopped directing plays altogether . . . I felt so betrayed.

135

WALTER

Betrayed? How did I betray you?

ELLIOT

By selling out!

WALTER

Grow up, Elliot. Selling out is a young person's idea. An adolescent's romantic notion that in order to be an artist you need to starve and suffer; commercial success is the devil's work. Well, I say, nuts to that.

ELLIOT

You were the paragon of artistic success!

WALTER

I was the paragon of nothing! I was a pragmatist who got sick of filling my calendar just to make enough to scrape by, and wanted to make some real money for a change!

ELLIOT

How does it feel knowing that you'll be best remembered for pandering to the puerile impulses of fifteen-year-old boys?

WALTER

It feels fine! If you think I've lost any sleep over this . . . I have nothing against fifteen-year-old boys; they're as legitimate a demographic as any. Fifteen-year-old boys have made me rich. I am indebted to them. Call it pandering if you like; I call it commerce. I provide a product to a vastly appreciative audience.

ELLIOT

My God. "Product." Listen to you! The old Walter would have been sick to his stomach.

136

WALTER

I *am* the old Walter! Same guy! I made this choice, long ago, no looking back, no regrets. What should I regret? The work on stage I didn't do? Not a chance. Starvation is not a virtue. I've tried it. It takes just as much energy and imagination making good, commercial entertainment than it does to make so-called art. So why not get paid for it? I discovered there will *always* be fifteen-year-old boys, an endless supply, *ad infinitum*, who go to the movies to watch all the cool different ways you can blow stuff up. I happen to like that, too.

ELLIOT

But what have you contributed to the world but pollution? At least when you worked in the theater . . .

WALTER

Ah, the thea-tuh, the thea-tuh. If I hear one more time how I abandoned the fucking thea-tuh . . . The grandiosity of theater people! Who have convinced themselves that what they do is of a higher order than all other forms of make-believe! What an odd pursuit, when you stop to think about it: Grown people shouting in rooms missing a fourth wall?

ELLIOT

Your *Winter's Tale* in the park . . . When Hermione came back to life . . .

WALTER

I hate to tell ya, that wasn't me, that was Shakespeare.

ELLIOT

It *was* you! It was beautiful!

WALTER

And where is it now, this beauty? Gone! Evaporated. The way of all ephemera.

ELLIOT

Ah, yes, what comfort that must bring: *Truck Stop 3* will live on and on!

WALTER

Mock me all you want. I am not going to apologize for its success. It's so easy for the smug wannabe to judge those who actually put themselves on the line and *make* things.
You're one to talk, Elliot. What have you done? Huh? Besides squander your life on vitriol. You've stewed in it. Remove the anger and what's left? Nothing! A big, fat void where a life should be!

(Elliot growls in rage and attacks Walter, knocking him to the floor.)

ELLIOT

Fuckin' son of a bitch! . . .

WALTER

My knee!

(Elliot gets on top of him.)

ELLIOT

Fuckin' piece a shit! . . .

(He has his hands around Walter's throat.)

WALTER

Get off me! Help! Get him the hell off me!

(Anna and Nell rush in from the kitchen. Pandemonium. The following happens very quickly.)

ANNA

Oh, my God! *(Calls)* Michael!

(Nell tries to help.)

NELL

Oh, shit! Elliot! Get off of him!

(Susie runs downstairs.)

SUSIE

Uncle Elliot! Stop!

(Michael runs in from the patio and tries to restrain Elliot.)

MICHAEL

Jesus, Elliot!

ANNA

Are you out of your mind?!

(Michael pries Elliot off Walter.)

MICHAEL

What the fuck is the matter with you?!

*(Elliot runs out of the house.
    Nell helps Walter upstairs. Michael and Susie go after Elliot.
Anna, shaken, returns to the kitchen.)*

SCENE 2

A few hours later. Late afternoon.
Nell comes downstairs with her luggage. Susie enters, sees
Nell, and decides to stay. She starts to straighten up the room.
Nell tries to help her.

SUSIE

I've got it.

NELL

I can do it.

(Susie tidies in silence.)

It looks like it's gonna rain again.

SUSIE

Are we going to talk about the weather?

NELL

I'm trying to make conver / sation.

SUSIE

Why bother? You're leaving.

NELL

Not right away. Your father needed to lie down. He was pretty
shaken up. Susie, / are you going to look at me?

SUSIE

Susan.

NELL

You avert your eyes whenever I look at you. Do you think you
can pretend I don't exist? Susie . . .

140

SUSIE

Susan!

NELL

You want me to treat you like an adult, then act like one!

SUSIE

You're not my mother . . .

NELL

I'm well aware of that.

(Pause.)

SUSIE

Look, I don't mean to be rude . . .

NELL

Oh, no?

SUSIE

Why did you come here?

NELL

To lend your dad moral support.

SUSIE

That thing last night with Michael: Is *that* how you lend moral support?

(Nell doesn't know what to say.)

You still plan on marrying my father?

NELL

Of course.

SUSIE

Why? He's old . . .

NELL

(Wearily) He's not old.

SUSIE

. . . Why would you want to be married to an old man?

NELL

That's not how I see him.

SUSIE

Maybe not now you don't. One day, tomorrow: A blood clot, a crack in the sidewalk, a knee replacement. He's old.

NELL

Age has nothing to do with it; bad stuff can happen to anyone at any age. Your mother was young, so there goes your theory.

SUSIE

Do you have a "daddy thing"?

NELL

What? No. I don't think so . . . Maybe I do.

SUSIE

What is *your* daddy like?

NELL

I didn't really know my dad.

SUSIE

Ah ha! Well, there you go. So you want mine.

142

NELL

I don't want your father. I want Walter Keegan. He'll still be your father.

SUSIE

Did you tell him what happened?

NELL

There was nothing to tell because nothing happened.

SUSIE

It sure *looked* like something happened.

NELL

That's not what it was.

SUSIE

Oh, no? What do *you* call it?

NELL

(Ashamed) Temporary insanity.

(Pause.)

SUSIE

Yeah.

(Pause.)

I know what Michael does to people.

NELL

What do you mean?

SUSIE

I've loved him my entire life.

NELL

You have?

SUSIE

I can remember seeing Michael's face when I was really, really young—I mean, *really* young—like in my crib—and thinking to myself—before I had words, even: This is a beautiful man. I swear. I remember that.

NELL

Y'know? You should be grateful I want to marry your father.

SUSIE

Why grateful?

NELL

Because some day he will be old. And he'll need taking care of, and *I'll* be the one doing the heavy lifting, not you.

SUSIE

Why are you signing on for this? I don't get it. What's in it for you? The money? You don't seem like the gold-digger type.

NELL

(Shrugs) It must be love.

SUSIE

Why would you want to be a part of this fucked-up family, anyway?

NELL

(Shrugs) That I couldn't tell you.

(Nell laughs. Susie looks at her.)

What.

SUSIE

You're so beautiful.

NELL

I'm not.

SUSIE

I can't even hate you for it because your beauty is so indisputable, it would be like hating sunsets. Did you know my mother?

(Nell shakes her head.)

Her movies don't do her justice. Her skin, she had such incredible skin. Even when she was dying, her skin was luminous. I had the worst zits from like twelve on, it was like a cruel joke that I should have this gorgeous movie-star mother who was perfection. It just wasn't fair. What must it be like to wake up every morning and see *that* in the mirror. *(Meaning: Nell's face)*

NELL

Are you *asking* me?

SUSIE

Yeah. How does it feel?

NELL

I don't feel beautiful.

SUSIE

I hate when beautiful people say that.

NELL

I don't, I mean it. I *never* felt beautiful. I was never very kind to myself.

I had an eating disorder till I was way in my twenties.

145

SUSIE

Really? You did?

NELL

Uh-huh. My dark secret. Now you know. Ruined my teeth. See?
All new veneers.

SUSIE

(Elated) Wow!

(Michael enters from the patio.)

MICHAEL

Hi.

NELL

Hi.

SUSIE

Still no sign of him?

MICHAEL

No.

SUSIE

I couldn't find him either.

MICHAEL

(To Nell) How's Walter?

NELL

Resting. I'm gonna throw this bag in the car.

(Nell takes her bag and goes.)

146

MICHAEL

I was hoping he showed up while I was out looking for him.

SUSIE

No.

MICHAEL

Say good-bye to him for me. Will you let me know he's all right?

SUSIE

Okay.

MICHAEL

Thanks.

(Susie starts to go.)

SUSIE

Well . . . see ya.

MICHAEL

Hey. C'mere.

(He gestures for her to come closer. She does, tentatively. He hugs her, kisses the top of her head.)

Love ya.

SUSIE

"Love ya" is the coward's way of saying "I love you." Love ya, too. Bye!

(She heads up the stairs. Nell returns.)

MICHAEL

(Calls) Susie. *(She stops)* Come see my show. Come opening night.

SUSIE

Yeah, sure. If I'm around.

(She's gone.)

NELL

I'm sorry I won't get to see you in *The Guardsman.*

MICHAEL

Don't be. Walter's right: Just me seeking absolution.

NELL

I should get him up.

MICHAEL

Nell . . . Listen. I, uh . . .

NELL

You don't have to say anything.

MICHAEL

I'm sorry.

NELL

I'm sorry. My mistake. I was curious. I should never have gone near you.

(She extends her hand.)

Good-bye, Michael.

(They shake hands. She starts to go upstairs.)

I hope you find what you're looking for.

(Anna enters from the garden with freshly cut flowers and sees them. Nell goes.)

148

ANNA

(To Michael) You're leaving.

MICHAEL

Yes.

ANNA

Where will you go?

MICHAEL

My place. I think it's safe for me to move in, finally.

ANNA

You're not worried about asphyxiation?

MICHAEL

The air should be clear by now.

ANNA

(Nods, then) That's not why you stayed on here, is it.

(He avoids eye contact.)

It was her. It was Nell. You stayed to be close to Nell.

You know? When I saw you in the market the other day . . .
posing for pictures by the organic fruit . . . I was transported,
instantly, back to a happier time. The years, age, death, everything disappeared. I was your Candida again.

MICHAEL

You're still sensational.

ANNA

Sweet of you to say. Tell me: Was I really so deluded, to think
I might have gotten some comfort from you? . . .

MICHAEL

Anna . . .

ANNA

. . . a little reassurance, from an old friend?

MICHAEL

I . . . didn't understand.

ANNA

What's not to understand? I thought it was obvious.

MICHAEL

What can I say? I'm not that smart.

ANNA

Hm. Maybe not. Here's a bit of advice, then: When a woman invites you into her home . . . and you don't seduce *her* . . . don't seduce *another* woman, darling, certainly not under the same roof. It's bad manners—ungallant to say the least.

MICHAEL

I never thought of you like that.

ANNA

Never?

MICHAEL

Well, not for a very long time.

ANNA

You mean now that my sell-by date has come and gone.

MICHAEL

That's not what I'm saying. I had a young man's crush on you. *I'm* the one who's changed.

ANNA

I could have seduced you all those years ago. But Kathy got you first. I could have gone all Mildred Pierce on you. But

I still had a modicum of dignity back then. Just a smidge. Now, apparently, not so much.

MICHAEL

I don't know who you think I am.

ANNA

I thought I knew.

MICHAEL

You've bought the press. I'm not some Lothario. I don't sleep with just anyone. I mean . . .

ANNA

Am I just anyone?

MICHAEL

I mean, I'm not cavalier.

ANNA

Oh. I see.

(Pause.)

Do you know what it's like being lit on a movie set for hours and hours because your eyes look like shit and no matter what the d.p. does your eyes *still* look like shit? There's only so much magic that lighting can do. Producers pace, and look at their watches, and shake their heads about how much this is costing them, and how beautiful I *used* to be. Do you have any idea what it's like to lose one's powers? Do you?

(He shakes his head.)

No. And you never will.

151

MICHAEL

Well . . .

(He comes closer to her.)

We're both gonna be up here for a while . . . Once I get settled, how about I cook for *you* for a change?

(She nods. Michael leans in to kiss her cheek. She kisses him full on the mouth.)

ANNA

All right, you may go now. Go! Your work here is done.

(Anna goes to the kitchen with the flowers.)

MICHAEL

(To himself) Jesus.

(He sees Elliot, soaking wet, enter from the garden.)

Hey. Where *were* you?

ELLIOT

Walking.

MICHAEL

Where?

ELLIOT

Around. In the woods.

MICHAEL

You're drenched.

ELLIOT

I needed to think.

MICHAEL

And?

ELLIOT

I had an epiphany.

MICHAEL

Yeah . . . ?

ELLIOT

My mother doesn't love me.

MICHAEL

What kind of shit is that? Of course your mother / loves you.

ELLIOT

Why "of course"? You think all women love their children?
Medea? Gertrude? Not all women should be mothers. It wasn't
a role that came naturally to her. She was miscast. And spent
all these years "indicating" like crazy: the least convincing
performance of her career.
    Did you know I had a stutter?

MICHAEL

I *didn't* / know that.

ELLIOT

I did. Something we don't talk about. I'm a recovering stutterer.
Like being an alcoholic: You're never really cured. Always one
consonant, one breath away from an avalanche.
    Whenever I spoke, I'd see Mother, clenched jaw, frozen
smile, staring into her salad, or down at her shoes, and imag-

153

ine her thinking, like a thought-bubble in a comic book: "Get on with it, Elliot, for God's sake, don't humiliate yourself, or more importantly, me." And I'd get so nervous, I'd lose traction and fly off the rails.

She set me up! Over and over again! She wanted me to fail!

MICHAEL

No she / didn't.

ELLIOT

She does it to this day! Whenever I open my mouth!

Listen to me: What a joke I am, huh? *(Mock tears)* "My mother doesn't love me."

MICHAEL

What are we gonna do with you, Elliot?

ELLIOT

You don't have to do anything.

(Michael hugs him. He reacts to Elliot's saturated clothing.)

MICHAEL

It's a good thing we're old friends, you know that?

ELLIOT

Oh, yeah? Why's that?

MICHAEL

Because if I just met you for the first time? . . . I wouldn't want to have anything to do with you.

ELLIOT

Thanks.

MICHAEL

Take care, buddy.

ELLIOT

You bet!

(Michael hoists his bag on his shoulder as Nell comes downstairs carrying Walter's suitcase. They exchange looks. Nell waves. Elliot observes them as Michael exits the house. She approaches Elliot.)

NELL

Listen: Elliot . . .

ELLIOT

Do me a favor? *(She nods)* If you're going to cheat on Walter, do it with me?

NELL

Listen: No matter how much you try to blame him for everything that's gone wrong in your life . . . Walter did not give Kathy cancer.

ELLIOT

She had a tremendous capacity for happiness, my sister. I marveled at her ability to put up with that man. She elevated him with her love.

NELL

Never mind.

ELLIOT

It kills me to see him landing another one of the world's great women.

(We hear Walter and Susie on the stairs.)

155

NELL

Good-bye, Elliot.

(Nell walks away.)

WALTER

(During the above) You think you'll make it home before the end of the summer?

SUSIE

At some point I will . . . I want to see my friends.

WALTER

Nell, honey, you about ready?

NELL

Yup.

SUSIE

(To Elliot) There you are. God.

(Walter looks at Elliot leerily.)

Talk to him.

ELLIOT

No.

(Elliot starts to go; Susie stops him.)

SUSIE

Dad? *(To Elliot)* Tell him you're sorry.

ELLIOT

I'm not sorry. What am I sorry for?

SUSIE

For behaving obnoxiously. Now tell him.

WALTER

Elliot, there's nothing you could possibly say / to me . . .

(Susie pushes Elliot toward Walter.)

ELLIOT

Hey!

(Susie gestures for him to speak.)

I'm sorry.

SUSIE

(Prompting) I'm sorry I behaved obnoxiously.

ELLIOT

I'm sorry I behaved obnoxiously.

WALTER

You didn't just behave obnoxiously, you had your hands around my throat.

ELLIOT

Fine. Forget it.

WALTER

There is a distinction. Your behaving obnoxiously I'm quite used to; being attacked physically, that's new and, frankly, worrisome. You've always been slightly unhinged. But in a lovably benign sort of way. Now you're fucking out of control.

(Pause.)

What's our plan, you and me? Hm? Is this how we're going to live out the rest of our lives? Sniping at each other? Let's not. God help us, but we're family, Elliot, whether we like it or not.

ELLIOT
Kathy was the best thing that ever happened to you.

WALTER
Don't you think I know that?

(Anna returns.)

ANNA
Oh, Walter, must you go?

WALTER
I think *so.*

ANNA
Everybody's leaving! When will I see you again?

WALTER
You'll come and see us in L.A.

(He hugs her.)

Good-bye, dear. Have fun with *Mrs. Warren.* You're going to be fabulous.

SUSIE
(To Walter) I'll walk you to your . . . Porsche.

(As Susie leads Walter out:)

ANNA
I still want your notes!

WALTER

I'll send them to you!

ANNA

Don't forget me!

WALTER

How could I?

(Susie and Walter are gone. Nell approaches Anna.)

NELL

Anna . . . Thank you so much.

ANNA

For what? A fiasco? It couldn't have gone much worse.

NELL

No, I suppose not. Next time we'll all be in better form.

ANNA

I should hope so. Good-bye, dear. Good luck with everything.

NELL

Thanks. You, too.

(Nell glances at Elliot as she heads out the door.)

ELLIOT

(Calls) Nell!

(She stops. A beat.)

We'll always have Louisville.

(Nell shakes her head and goes. Anna and Elliot are alone. Silence.)

ANNA

Happy now?

ELLIOT

Hm?

ANNA

You got what you wanted. You drove them all away.

ELLIOT

Oh, and you had nothing to do with this farce?

ANNA

Me?! What did *I* do?

ELLIOT

Not only do you let Walter bring his new girlfriend: the only woman I ever loved . . .

ANNA

How was *I* to know / that?

ELLIOT

But Michael?!

ANNA

What *about* / Michael?

ELLIOT

Flinging yourself at him / like that?

ANNA

I don't know what you're talking about. Michael could be my son.

ELLIOT

Exactly. How icky is that? Shame on you. Trying to get a mercy fuck out of Michael.

ANNA

How *dare* you . . . ! What an outrageous thing to say!

ELLIOT

So much for the grieving mother.

ANNA

(Enraged) Are you questioning my grief?! Are you? *She was my child!* She may have been *your* sister but she was *my child!* I will not quantify my suffering because of some primitive notion you have of how I should or should not conduct myself. You don't know what it's like to lose a child. You have no idea. If having Walter and Michael here made me feel closer to Kathy, so be it!

(Silence.)

ELLIOT

I wish it had been me, Mother. I so wish / it had been me.

ANNA

Oh for God's sake . . .

ELLIOT

I should have been the one who died. An early death would have lent my life a little dignity, y'know?, a touch of tragedy. It would have been so much better all around.

ANNA

What a childish / thing to say.

161

ELLIOT

Oh, come on, don't pretend you haven't thought it.

(She turns away. Pause.)

Look at me, Mama. *(He waits for her to face him)* How did this happen to me? How did I become this . . . sad excuse for a man? I wasted so much time! On what? Auditions! Rehearsals for living, not living. Kathy dies. My magnificent sister. Of lung cancer! Never smoked a day in her life. But I, with my self-destructive habits and . . . *mediocrity*, get to go on breathing? Why? It doesn't make sense.

ANNA

You know, dear, I've often thought you cultivated bad habits just to make yourself more interesting.

ELLIOT

I don't interest you. Do I?

ANNA

I'm not going to play this game.

ELLIOT

(Prosecutorially) Do I interest you? Answer the question.

ANNA

No, my dear. You do not.

ELLIOT

You could at least make a show of protest.

ANNA

You haven't interested me in quite some time.

ELLIOT

Nice.

ANNA

Watching you flail about. How do you think that made me *feel*?

ELLIOT

Made *you* feel?!

ANNA

It was torture—torture!—sitting by helplessly while you failed time and time again.

(Silence.)

ELLIOT

All my life . . . I've been the only nobody in the room. I have dropped your name to people I wanted to like me. Directors have cast me in plays hoping *you'd* show up opening night— which, of course, you never did.

ANNA

If I *could* have, of course / I would have come.

ELLIOT

I had promise. Once. *(À la Brando)* "I coulda been a contenda. I coulda been somebody." Comedy! I did improv at school. But you never came to see me! You were always working.

ANNA

I *was* / always working.

ELLIOT

I was good! I was funny! If only you had seen for yourself! But, no, you didn't come, / you assumed I'd be bad.

163

ANNA

I *couldn't* come because I was working.

ELLIOT

Kathy you saw in every damn thing she was in. If she was one of a multitude of *sugarplum fairies*, you were there!

ANNA

Listen to your / self!

ELLIOT

Would it have taken so much to offer me even the slightest bit of encouragement? Would it? You were so . . . withholding, so stingy. As if offering praise meant giving up a vital part of yourself. If only you had told me I was good at *some*thing! Instead you told me I was hopeless, there was nothing I did well.

ANNA

I never said you were hopeless!

ELLIOT

You may as well have.

ANNA

I didn't want you to get your hopes *up*. That's not the same thing.

ELLIOT

How could you deprive your child of hope?! It's unnatural.

ANNA

I was protecting you!

ELLIOT

Protecting me?!

ANNA

So you wouldn't be disappointed.

(Long pause.)

ELLIOT

Y'know . . . ? When I was a boy . . . and you'd go off to the theater? . . . I'd wait up for you to come home, force myself to stay awake till one or two in the morning. My heart would pound when I'd hear your keys jingle and your footsteps in the hall, and pray you'd come in to kiss me. You'd breeze in, in the dark, smelling like night, cold cream on your cheek. I'd lay there pretending to be asleep because I knew that if you found out I waited up, you would stop coming in and that would be that. I spent years at grade school exhausted from lack of sleep—until one night you discovered my gambit and those good-night kisses came to an end.

I'm still that boy in the dark, praying for your kiss.

ANNA

Darling, I . . .

(Elliot, crying, drops to his knees, clutches his mother around her legs.)

ELLIOT

Oh, Mama . . .

ANNA

(Trying to walk away) What are you doing?

ELLIOT

Please, Mama, don't walk away!

ANNA

Get up! Let go of me!

(She pushes him away; he remains on the floor. We hear a car on gravel. Susie returns, assesses the situation but doesn't address it.)

Are they gone?

SUSIE

(Nods) All gone.

(Pause. Thunder.)

ANNA

Is this rain ever going to stop?

SUSIE

Uncle Elliot?

ELLIOT

Yeah?

SUSIE

The man in your play who kills himself . . . He's you, right?

ELLIOT

Not necessar / ily.

SUSIE

Don't be coy; he *is* you.

(He shrugs.)

You'd rather be dead? Is that what you're saying?

166

ELLIOT

I'm saying . . . I can understand what it must be like to be in so much pain, you'd do whatever it takes to make it stop.

SUSIE

You really believe that?

(Elliot nods.)

(Emotionally) Why would you say that to me?

ELLIOT

What?

SUSIE

I see you killing yourself, slowly. And it's terrible.

ANNA

Oh, darling . . .

SUSIE

Watching you seethe and drink and you're so jealous of other people's happiness. If you're unhappy you don't want anyone else to be happy, either. You lost your faith a long time ago, I know. And when Mom got sick, it gave you like all the proof you needed that everything was shit. But she would hate to see you like this, Uncle Elliot, she'd hate to see what you're doing to yourself and everybody else. Please. Try to have a little faith. For me. For Mom.

(Susie joins him on the floor, leaning against the couch.)

ELLIOT

She was my best friend.

SUSIE	ANNA
I know.	Yes, she was.

ELLIOT

Yin to my yang. Gretel to my Hansel. I have nobody now.

ANNA

That's not true. Of course you do.

ELLIOT

Nobody who loves me unconditionally, not like she did. Who do I have?

SUSIE

You have *me* . . . Idiot.

Remember that? When I was little? I called you Uncle Idiot?

ELLIOT

(Laughing) Uncle Idiot. Yes. Who knew how prophetic?

SUSIE

I thought it was the most hilarious thing in the world.

(He pulls her closer to him and kisses her forehead. Anna gets the photo album and sets it down near Susie and Elliot.

She sits near them but can't bring herself to look at the photos with them.)

(Regarding a photo) That's this room. *(Elliot nods)* How come there's no furniture in it?

ANNA

We hadn't moved in yet. We hadn't even put a bid on it yet. We were looking at the house for the first time. Elliot and Kathy were so excited, they ran through all the rooms and up and down stairs. That clinched it for Leonard and me: We could see ourselves being so happy here.

SUSIE

(Another photo) God, look how cute she was. You know? *I* kind of looked like that when I was that age.

ANNA

Uh-huh. You did.

SUSIE

(Another photo) Why were you dressed like that?

ELLIOT

It was our Christmas play. I was Joseph. See? Your mom was the Virgin Mary.

SUSIE

Who are they?

ELLIOT

Oh, just some cousins who were staying with us. Whoever happened to be visiting got to be donkeys and camels. We stopped doing it the year Dad left.

SUSIE

Gran, tell about the time Mom and Uncle Elliot surprised you for your birthday.

ANNA

For *my* birthday?

SUSIE

Yeah. Mom told me. You were up here doing a play?

ANNA

What play was I doing?

SUSIE

I don't remember. You were in rehearsal and a call came?

ANNA

From whom?

ELLIOT

From me.

ANNA

Saying what?

ELLIOT

"Kathy's scared! Come home right away!" *(To Susie)* There was a thunderstorm. She *hated* thunderstorms, your mom.

ANNA

And what did I do?

ELLIOT

You came home.

ANNA

I left rehearsal?!

ELLIOT

Uh-huh.

ANNA

When have I *ever* left rehearsal?

ELLIOT

You did. You were in costume.

ANNA

What was I wearing? *(Thinks, then)* Oh! I was doing Nora!
I was wearing my dress for the tarantella! Yes, and I got in
the car, raced to the house, and ran inside calling, "*Kathyyy!*"
And out she popped, from behind the sofa—that little imp—
"Surprise!" It was all a ruse! I was furious!

(She slips down on the floor near Elliot.)

And then came Elliot, holding the saddest, flattest, home-
baked birthday cake, candles blazing, and the two of them
sang "Happy Birthday" and my anger . . . went away. We blew
out the candles and plopped ourselves down, right here, the
three of us, and tore into that chocolate cake—with our *fin-
gers!*—and talked . . . and laughed . . . and ate it all up, we
devoured it, till there was nothing left on the plate but crumbs!

*(Elliot and Susie slide closer to Anna. She leans in closer and
the three of them begin to look at the album together as the
lights fade completely to black.)*

END OF PLAY

DONALD MARGULIES received the 2000 Pulitzer Prize for Drama for *Dinner with Friends* (Variety Arts Theatre, New York; Comedie des Champs-Elysées, Paris; Hampstead Theatre, London; Actors Theatre of Louisville; South Coast Repertory, Costa Mesa). The play received numerous awards, including the American Theatre Critics Association New Play Award, The Dramatists Guild/Hull-Warriner Award, the Lucille Lortel Award, the Outer Critics Circle Award and a Drama Desk nomination.

His many plays include *Time Stands Still* (commissioned and co-produced by the Geffen Playhouse, Los Angeles, and Manhattan Theatre Club, New York), which was a Tony Award nominee for Best Play); *Coney Island Christmas* (based on the short story "The Loudest Voice" by Grace Paley; commissioned and produced by the Geffen Playhouse); *Shipwrecked! An Entertainment—The Amazing Adventures of Louis de Rougemont (As Told by Himself)* (commissioned and produced by South Coast Repertory, Costa Mesa; Geffen Playhouse; Primary Stages); *Brooklyn Boy* (commissioned and produced by South Coast Repertory; Manhattan Theatre Club; Comedie des Champs-Elysées), which was an American Theatre Critics Association New Play Award finalist and an Outer Critics Circle nominee; *Sight Unseen* (commissioned and produced by South Coast Repertory; Manhattan Theatre Club; Comedie des Champs-Elysées), which received an OBIE Award; *Collected Stories* (Theatre Royal Haymarket, London; South Coast Repertory; Manhattan Theatre Club; HB Studio/Lucille Lortel Theatre, New York), which received the Los Angeles Drama Critics Circle/Ted Schmitt Award, the L.A. Ovation Award, a Drama Desk nomination, and which was a finalist for The Dramatists Guild/Hull-Warriner Award and the Pulitzer Prize; *God of Vengeance* (based on the Yiddish classic by Sholom Asch; produced by ACT Theatre, Seattle; Williamstown Theatre Festival, Massachusetts); *Two Days* (Long Wharf Theatre, New Haven); *The Model Apartment* (Los Angeles Theatre Center; Primary Stages; La Jolla Playhouse; Long Wharf Theatre), which won an OBIE Award, a Drama-Logue Award, and was a Dramatists Guild/Hull-Warriner Award finalist and a Drama Desk nominee; *The Loman Family Picnic* (Manhattan Theatre Club), which was a Drama Desk nominee; *What's Wrong with This Picture?* (Manhattan Theatre Club; Jewish Repertory Theatre, New York; Brooks Atkinson Theatre, New York); *Broken Sleep: Three Plays* (Williamstown Theatre Festival); July 7, 1994 (Actors Theatre of Louisville); *Found a Peanut* (The Joseph Papp Public Theater/New York Shakespeare Festival); *Pitching to the Star* (West Bank Café, New York); *Resting Place* (Theatre for the New City, New York); *Gifted Children*; *Zimmer* and *Luna Park* (Jewish Repertory Theatre).

Dinner with Friends was made into an Emmy Award–nominated film for HBO, and *Collected Stories* was presented on PBS.

Mr. Margulies has received grants from the National Endowment for the Arts, the New York Foundation for the Arts, and the John Simon Guggenheim Memorial Foundation. He was the recipient of the 2015 William Inge Distinguished Achievement in the American Theater Award, the 2014 PEN/Laura Pels International Foundation for Theater Award for an American Playwright in Mid-Career, and the 2000 Sidney

Kingsley Award for Outstanding Achievement in the Theatre by a Playwright. In 2005 he was honored by the American Academy of Arts and Letters with an Award in Literature and by the National Foundation for Jewish Culture with its Award in Literary Arts. Mr. Margulies is an alumnus of New Dramatists and serves on the council of The Dramatists Guild of America.

Born in Brooklyn, New York, in 1954, Mr. Margulies now lives with his wife, Lynn Street, a physician, and their son, Miles, in New Haven, Connecticut, where he is an adjunct professor of English and Theatre Studies at Yale University.